HAVE CLUBS, WILL TRAVEL

Fore! Linda
your friend in golf.
Marilyn Smith
2018

HAVE CLUBS, WILL TRAVEL

Marilynn Smith

with Bob Cayne

ap

Ambassador
Publishing

2012

Published by Ambassador Publishing

Ambassador Publishing
3784 N 162nd Lane
Goodyear, AZ 85395

www.marilynnsmith.com

www.lpga.com

Library of Congress Cataloging-In-Publication Data

Smith, Marilynn   Biography   Sports

ISBN: 978-0-615-67728-6

Printed in the United States of America

1 2 3 4 5 6 7 8 9

This book is dedicated to:

My parents, Alma and Lynn Smith

My grandmother, Lillian Fogg

My sister and brother-in-law, Gay and Clifford Pappas

My fifth grade teacher, Iva Malone

My first golf teacher, Mike Murra, PGA

My friend, Colonel Pat Grant, Retired

My friend, Debbie Waitkus

The LPGA co-founders, and the LPGA

Contents

Contents

CONTENTS

Acknowledgments

I would like to thank my family and friends who have encouraged me to document and write my memoirs. Some offered input, reviewed the manuscript and provided valuable comments. I am grateful for their feedback and the interest they have shown in this project.

Thanks also to the LPGA for supporting the Marilynn Smith Scholarship Fund and for many other ways they have been there for me. To my fellow LPGA co-founders and tour players who inspire me with their talent and whose colorful personalities gave me material for this book, I say thank you. It came to fruition because of you and our collective passion for golf.

I must recognize Tom Quinlan, chief executive officer of RR Donnelley & Sons Company for his generous assistance in printing this book and for his financial support of the RR Donnelley Founders Cup. We are grateful to our sponsors, they are the reason the LPGA has been able to grow and prosper over the years.

Others who contributed by jogging my memory, editing and supplying photographs include Shirley Spork, whose stories about our days traveling together appear on these pages; Jack Mishler, who helped organize the photographs and Mary Ann Souter, who researched and assembled historical data that formed the book's framework.

Finally, Bob Cayne made it all come to life. He and I wrote and we edited—again and again. I'm proud of the end result.

Foreword

Writing a forward for Marilynn Smith's memoirs is easy and a pleasure for me. I always enjoy talking about the Founders of the LPGA whenever possible, and thank them for making the LPGA what it is today. In addition, I thank them for giving me the opportunity to have a career I truly loved.

When I joined the tour in 1959, Marilynn was the president of the LPGA. For a young and very inexperienced player, Marilynn was perfect. She was, and still is, very friendly. She always has a smile for you. In fact, one of her nicknames was "Smiley" and it fit her perfectly.

The LPGA was very fortunate to have Marilynn as president because the president contracted for tournaments and met with prospective sponsors in the early years. In other words, she was our commissioner! Blessed with her personality, love for golf and belief in the LPGA, we got off to a great start.

In addition to her duties and the way she constantly promoted the LPGA, Marilynn was an excellent player. She took her game seriously and was always on the practice tee tying to get better. She won 21 tournaments, including two majors.

Foreword

In 2006, Marilynn asked me to present her for induction to the World Golf Hall of Fame. What an honor and pleasure it was to be able to present this great lady to the world of golf.

As you read about Marilynn's life, you will be able to better understand why so many of us hold her in very high regard as a person, founder and professional golfer.

Again, Marilynn, thank you so much for all you have done for the game of golf.

Kathy Whitworth

Flower Mound, Texas

Preface

I'm just an ordinary person from the Kansas prairie who has lived an extraordinary life. Where but in America—and all because of golf—could a gal from Kansas travel to all 50 states, 37 countries, six continents, meet five United States presidents and play golf with her two idols, Ben Hogan and Stan Musial?

I was fortunate to be an LPGA co-founder; to collaborate with women determined to succeed in professional golf. We may have been dreamers, but we did, indeed, earn a living as tournament players and beyond as teaching professionals. Our individuality, charisma and capabilities benefited the organization, for we were a player-run tour without a weak link. I hope these pages do justice to their contributions. They kept us afloat in the early days.

The 13 Founders are Babe Didrikson Zaharias, Patty Berg, Alice and Marlene Bauer, Helen Hicks, Shirley Spork, Louise Suggs, Sally Sessions, Opal Hill, Helen Dettweiler, Betty Jameson, Bettye Danoff and, me.

How times have changed. In 1950, we started with 13 events and $50,000 in prize money. By 1968, the organization had grown to 40 players, 33 events and $550,000. In 2012, touring LPGA members are playing for $47 million in prize money. What began as a baker's dozen has grown to more than 2,000 members from all over the world.

I've tried to capture the excitement and enthusiasm, the struggles, emotions and anecdotes from the early days and from my life as a professional golfer. I am most grateful and honored to share my story with you.

Growing Up in Kansas

Baseball. I lived and breathed baseball from the time I was 10 years old. I was going to pitch for the St. Louis Cardinals, throw shutouts, baffle hitters, and play in the World Series. It didn't matter that I was a girl, I dreamed I'd be a professional baseball player someday and I was preparing for my future by playing on a local boys' team in Wichita.

I did it all. I was the pitcher, coach and manager. Each week I climbed into my baseball uniform and rushed to the field, eager to play, anxious to improve. Before the game I sucked on a lemon because somebody told me it was a good thing to do. To this day I have no idea why. Maybe it was a superstition.

I was a good pitcher. Not a hurler, a pitcher, with a mean knuckle ball that seemed to float. Batters waved at it. If they started looking for the knuckler I fed them fastballs, ones they had a tough time catching up with. I felt confident, knowing that hard work and continued improvement would eventually earn me a place on a major league roster.

Of course, long-term goals don't always work out. At least, mine didn't. After one memorable game, a tough loss, my mother, who was always interested in my activities, asked, "How did you do today?" I was upset and the question hit a nerve. I reacted foolishly and without thinking. I slammed my glove against the wall and summed up the day with a four-letter word I learned on the sandlots. Boy, did that light a fuse. My mother marched me to the sink and washed my mouth out with Lifebuoy soap. Ugh, but that was the way kids were punished for mouthing off to their parents.

When my dad came home my mother told him about my outburst. He said, "Well, dear, we had better take her to Wichita Country Club to learn a more ladylike sport."

Looking back, profanity introduced me to golf. It can get a player tossed off a golf course but, in my case, it jump-started a lifelong career.

At first I thought golf was a 'sissy' sport. Who wants to hit a ball and chase after it? Fortunately, my dad excelled at attitude adjustments. He said he would buy me a bicycle if I could break 40 for nine holes. What incentive. I did my best, and before long I was peddling to the course on a brand new Schwinn with my golf bag on my back. I was sold on the game and particularly enjoyed playing with my dad. It was a special time for us. I remember our mornings together on the golf course; how he encouraged and inspired me.

Mike Murra, the head pro at Wichita Country Club was a true gentleman who wore a shirt and tie when he gave golf lessons. He was patient and understanding. I was the only girl in his Saturday morning boy's class, but after a few weeks Mike recognized my natural talent for the game and offered to give me private lessons. My game improved rapidly and, with it, my confidence. Mike Murra made me a golfer; he played an important role in my decision to pursue a golf career.

I took away from my childhood a respect for others. I mean, look how abruptly my parents and Mike changed my life. They steered me in a direction I may never have found by myself. I didn't set out to be a golfer, certainly not with the skills to compete on a national level as a *teenager*.

But, I'm getting ahead of myself.

In 1948, after graduating from high school, I was accepted at the University of Kansas. The school didn't have a girl's golf team, but my father asked Phog Allen, the athletic director, if expense money was available so I could play in the Women's Intercollegiate Golf Tournament in Columbus, Ohio. "Mr. Smith," he said, "it's too bad your daughter isn't a boy." Fortunately, dad was able to take me.

I had a good tournament. In the semifinal match I defeated Alice O'Neal, the 1946 Indiana state champion, 6-and-5, but lost in the finals, 2-down to Grace Lenczyk.

Golf World was impressed with my performance. In the tournament story they ran my picture with this cutline:

Miss Marilynn Smith (For future Reference)

They were going to keep an eye on me.

The next year, I won the Women's National Intercollegiate Golf Tournament at Ohio State University's famous Scarlet Course beating the defending champion, Grace Lenczyk who was also the reigning U.S. Amateur Champion from Florida's Stetson University.

The newspaper story said:

The smilin' Smitty from the sunflower state clowned her way into the hearts of all tournament followers, but she was strictly serious through the final match.

When the match ended on the sixteenth green, Smitty shook hands with Miss Lenczyk and made the usual courtesy gestures. But when she greeted her father, the storm broke. She let go with all the pent-up emotion and nervousness and sobbed uncontrollably.

Then, back at the clubhouse her old smiling and kid personality self again, Smitty was called to the phone to talk with her mother long-distance. Mrs. Smith heard the news and cried for joy. Smitty joined her.

That was a magic moment for me and, as it turned out, a springboard to the professional ranks.

Golf World had a scoop:

Marilynn Smith won the 1949 trophy and immediately turned professional to work for Spalding Brothers.

Well, that was correct, but turning pro was far from a spur of the moment thing. The process began long before the 1949 tournament when George Dawson, A. G. Spalding Brothers Sporting Goods Company vice president, played in a tournament at Wichita Country Club and Mike Murra told him about his 19-year-old protégé. "She's won three straight Kansas State Amateur titles," he said. "You should take a look at her."

Before long Mr. Dawson was in our living room discussing a proposal for me to turn professional and join Spalding's staff. Dad was all for it. He stressed that "opportunity may only knock once." After two years at the University of Kansas, I faced a tough choice: finish college or turn pro. I was only 19-years old, unprepared for such a life-changing decision.

Several prayerful nights passed—many hours of parental counsel. My interests in college leaned toward politics or teaching. But my tournament success overshadowed all that. Deep down I knew I was a golfer. In the end, dad's wisdom was the deciding factor. I took the offer.

I actually turned professional several weeks before signing with Spalding. I was somewhat apprehensive, but those three consecutive Kansas amateur championships formed the foundation for a golf career. I wanted to make a living playing the game I loved.

Dad drove Grace Lenczyk and me to Oklahoma City for the Women's Western Open. When I registered as a pro the ladies at the desk were shocked. "Are you sure?" they asked. They were baffled, with good reason. Lady golfers rarely turned pro. Raising the question was a sign of the times.

Ladies didn't turn pro because there was a World War II backlash against women who worked for a living. We weren't supposed to make the sports page. "Rosie the Riveter," (a fictional character used by the government to promote the war effort's importance), received a pat on the back for helping to win the war. Then she was told to get back to the kitchen as rapidly as possible. Independent career women were viewed suspiciously; professional female athletes led the list. It took us a long time to gain respect. Women were expected to get married and have children or, in my case, finish college.

The Women's Western Open launched my professional career and with it, my life changed in ways I could never imagine.

In July, I took the Santa Fe Railroad from Wichita, to the Spalding factory in Chicopee, Massachusetts. It was a long train trip, but I was afraid to fly. I wanted to arrive in one piece so I could sign the first in what turned out to be 27 one-year contracts. (That beats Walter Alston's 23 one-year contracts with the Dodgers.) My relationship with Spalding was excellent; it relieved whatever apprehension the Western Open experience may have caused.

They gave me a $5,000 annual salary, an unlimited expense account and a forest-green Dodge Coronet. Spalding also promised to market Marilynn Smith women's golf clubs. "Another thing," I said before signing, (old habits are hard to break), "Throw in a couple gloves and a baseball so I can play catch with the caddies." That sealed the deal.

Spalding kept me busy. My job was to represent them by playing in tournaments, giving clinics and conducting exhibitions. I promoted golf throughout the United States and abroad.

My appearances were at Spalding's key accounts: country clubs, golf clubs and colleges. District salesmen made all the arrangements.

My corporate affiliation was far from groundbreaking. Babe Zaharias and Patty Berg represented Wilson Sporting Goods, Louise Suggs was with MacGregor Golf and Shirley Spork represented Golfcraft. Much earlier, in the 1930s, Helen Hicks, Opal Hill and Helen Dettweiler were Wilson players. There was ample precedence.

Spalding never pressured me to win. Mr. Dawson merely asked that I play as well as I could. Promoting the game as a Spalding staff member came first. I was a fortunate young lady. My timing was perfect. I was in the right place at the right time.

You know, Lifebuoy soap didn't taste all that bad.

Shaping the Future of Women's Golf

In 1944, three golfers organized the first official women's golf tour: the Women's Professional Golf Association (WPGA).

Hope Seignious was the driving force, the brains behind idea. She served as secretary-treasurer and tournament director. Betty Hicks, the 1941 amateur champion, was president. Ellen Griffin, a physical education professor at the University of North Carolina's Women's College, was vice president.

Before long, well-known players like Helen Dettweiler, Kathryn Hemphill and Betty Jameson joined the group. The WPGA only lasted from 1944 to 1949, but it was the foundation on which the LPGA would be built.

In 1946, Hope Seignious, persuaded the Spokane Athletic Round Table—a fraternal organization that enjoyed significant income from *slot machine proceeds*—to put up $19,700 in war bonds for the first Women's Open. Who could have predicted *that*? Patty Berg won the event—and $5,600 in bonds—defeating Betty Jameson, 5-and-4, in the 36-hole championship match.

It was the only time the Women's Open would be match play.

Hope funded the next two Women's Opens—at Starmount Forest Country Club in Greensboro, North Carolina and Atlantic City Country Club in Atlantic City, New Jersey—with her own savings. Betty Jameson won in 1947, Babe Zaharias in 1948.

It's worth noting: The U.S. Women's Open is the only USGA championship that was started by an outside organization—testimony to Hope's entrepreneurial vision.

She also started winter tournaments and encouraged amateur events to add purses. To name a few: Hardscrabble in Fort Smith, Arkansas; the Tam O'Shanter in Chicago; the George S. May World Open; the Tampa Open; the Texas and Western Opens and the Titleholders Championship in Augusta.

Hope's dream may have failed for lack of finances, but her legacy includes the LPGA guidelines and the Women's National Open. The LPGA retained the Open for four years, then, in 1953, the United States Golf Association—at the LPGA's request—adopted the tournament and renamed it the U.S. Women's Open Championship, one of the world's showcase athletic events.

Betty Hicks, a member of the WPGA and later the LPGA, didn't think the WPGA's eventual failure was a reflection on Hope Seignious' leadership. "Hope was very innovative," she said. "She organized the early tournaments for us. Unfortunately, too many players thought all they had to do was play and didn't help out in other ways. I finally left the WPGA in 1948 to go back to college at San Jose State. I figured the way I was playing I was going to need a second career."

Patty Berg had great respect for Seignious. "We had vision, great ideas," she said. "But we were able to operate for just so long. We had to keep the American public with us and we couldn't, despite the marvelous contributions of Hope, Betty and Ellen Griffin."

L.B. Icely, president of Wilson Sporting Goods, who was widely credited with leading the company through its most creative period, came to the rescue. He contacted Fred Corcoran and said, "If I can get the other manufacturers to join in, will you set up a tournament schedule for the lady pros?" Corcoran agreed and Wilson, along with Spalding and MacGregor funded his new position.

Corcoran had previously managed the PGA of America's pro tour. At one point Sam Snead won the Oakland Open but decided to skip the Phoenix Open because he could collect guaranteed money by playing exhibitions. Fred—an enterprising person if there ever was one—stepped in and became Snead's manager. Ted

Williams, who was on Wilson's advisory staff, and Stan Musial were also Corcoran clients. Same deal.

Mildred "Babe" Zaharias' was his newest client. Women golf pros made their living by teaching or giving clinics and playing exhibitions under the auspices of an equipment manufacturer. Babe drew national attention for her golfing skills when Fred arranged for her to be the first woman to play in a PGA Tour event, the Los Angeles Open. He booked her into baseball stadiums for $500 a night. She played golf exhibitions and toured with Gene Sarazan. By 1948, Babe's income from miscellaneous sports exceeded $100,000, but her tournament golf winnings were less than $3,500.

Fred's promotional skills were evident; there was little doubt that he could help women's golf.

His first recommendation was to change the name to the Ladies Professional Golf Players Association. The change was made at the 1949 Women's Eastern Open and Corcoran was named tournament manager. The new association members were Patty Berg, Betty Mims Danoff, Helen Dettweiler, Helen Hicks, Betty Jameson and Babe Zaharias. Patty was the association's first president.

The Ladies Professional Golf Association

This is where it all began. The 1950 U.S. Women's Open was played from September 27 to 30 at Rolling Hills Country Club in Wichita, my hometown. On the day of the final round, the Ladies Professional Golf Players Association (LPGPA) was reorganized and incorporated as the Ladies Professional Golf Association of America (LPGA). Patty Berg, Helen Dettweiler, Sally Sessions, Betty Jameson and Helen Hicks signed the incorporation papers.

The charter members were: Patty Berg, Alice Bauer, Marlene Bauer, Betty Mims Danoff, Helen Dettweiler, Opal Hill, Betty Jameson, Sally Sessions, Marilynn Smith, Shirley Spork, Louise Suggs and Babe Zaharias. Patty was president; Helen vice president; Betty treasurer and Sally secretary.

Wilson, Spalding and MacGregor continued to underwrite Fred Corcoran's salary. He scheduled events and tournament activities for another two years at LPGA headquarters in New York City. Spec Hammond handled pairings, the scoreboard and other tournament duties.

In 1950, we played 13 events with $50,000 total prize money. Babe Zaharias was the leading money winner, earning $14,800 with six wins.

To put things in perspective, the average annual income was $3,216. Gasoline cost 18 cents a gallon; bacon was 35 cents a pound. You could buy a new car for $1,500, a loaf of bread for 14 cents. T-bone steaks cost 59 cents a pound.

The co-founders came from various parts of the country and different backgrounds. Our personalities ran the gamut. I guess you could call us trailblazers who were willing to travel 40,000 miles a year playing golf and promoting the LPGA.

But the first order of business was: Get the organization up and running.

Betsy Rawls said, "I believe the LPGA set standards, not only for women's golf, but for women's organizations, professional and amateur. The Association has led the movement toward total acceptance and even financial success for women athletes traveling toward the twenty-first century."

HAVE CLUBS, WILL TRAVEL

CERTIFICATE OF INCORPORATION

OF

LADIES' PROFESSIONAL GOLF ASSOCIATION OF AMERICA, INC.

Pursuant to the Membership Corporations Law

WE, THE UNDERSIGNED, for the purpose of forming a membership corporation pursuant to the Membership Corporations Law of the State of New York, hereby certify:

1. The name of the proposed corporation shall be LADIES' PROFESSIONAL GOLF ASSOCIATION OF AMERICA, INC.

2. The purposes for which it is to be formed are:

To elevate the standards of the women's professional golfers' vocation; to promote interest among women in the game of golf; to protect the mutual interests of its members; to hold meetings and tournaments periodically for the encouragement of the members; to voluntarily assist deserving members who may be out of employment to obtain a position; to institute a benevolent fund for the voluntary relief of deserving members.

3. The territory in which its operations are principally to be conducted is the United States, its territories and possessions.

4. The city and county in which its office is to be located are the City, County and State of New York.

5. The number of its directors shall be not less than three nor more than eleven.

6. The names and residences of the directors until the first annual meeting are:

Patty Berg, Wilson Sporting Goods Co., Chicago, Ill

Helen Dettweiler, Box 3437, Indio, California

Sally Sessions, 18698 Schaefer, Detroit, Mich.

Betty Jameson, 258 Watalen, San Antonio, Texas

Helen Hicks, 812 Central Avenue, Woodmere, L.I., N.Y.

7. All the subscribers to this Certificate are of full age. At least two-thirds of them are citizens of the United States; at least one of them is a resident of the State of New York. Of the persons named as directors, at least one is a citizen of the United States and a resident of the State of New York.

IN WITNESS WHEREOF, we have made, subscribed and acknowledged this Certificate this 30th day of September 1950, and 9th day of October 1950.

(s) Patty Berg

(s) Helen Dettweiler

(s) Sally Sessions

(s) Betty Jameson

(s) Helen Hicks

812 Central Ave.

Woodmere,

Long Island, New York

The Founders

When LPGA Commissioner Mike Whan was in Phoenix for the 2011 Founders Cup tournament he partnered with Shirley Spork, 83, in the pro-am. After play, Mike said, "The best part of my day was listening to Shirley pass along her knowledge of the organization's early years. Sometimes, we go from tournament to tournament forgetting how it all started."

These are the women who started it. They are the Founders:

Alice Bauer and her sister Marlene Bauer Hagge came from Eureka, South Dakota.

 When Alice was 14 years old she was voted South Dakota's Outstanding Female Athlete of the year. When she was 15, she won the Long Beach Invitational—and proceeded to win it six consecutive times. At age 22 she was an LPGA co-founder. Galleries gasped watching her clubhead almost hit the ground on her l-o-n-g backswing. Alice played a limited tour schedule because her two young children were her first priority.

 Marlene began her golf career at 3-1/2. She was Shirley Temple in spikes. She starred in California amateur

17

events; became the youngest player to make the cut in a U.S. Women's Open when she was 13; turned professional and began her LPGA career at age 16. She won 26 tournaments—eight in 1956, alone—and one major, the 1956 LPGA Championship. Marlene played competitively through five decades.

 Patty Berg, from Minneapolis, Minnesota, was a lieutenant in the Marine Corps during World War II. That experience helped her lead us in our formative years. She won 28 amateur tournaments in seven years. Patty was one of six inaugural inductees into the LPGA Hall of Fame. Her records and accomplishments, if accumulated in the modern era would make her a zillionaire. In 1955, Patty was the Associated Press Woman Athlete of the Year after she led the LPGA in both earnings and scoring. She was named "Golfer of the Decade" for the period 1938-1947 by *GOLF* magazine. Patty still holds the women's record for most majors won: 15 (one U.S. Women's Open, seven Titleholders and seven Western Opens).

 We called Bettye Mims Danoff "Mighty Mite." She belted the ball a long way for a little gal with a compact swing. Bettye came from Dallas. She won four straight Dallas Women's Golf Association Championships, the Women's Division of the Texas PGA two times, and the Texas Women's Amateur two times. She and Alice Bauer

were the first players to take their children on tour. Years later, she was the first grandmother on tour. Her 1947 Texas Open victory was significant—it ended Babe Zaharias' 17-event winning streak.

 Helen Dettweiler served in World War II. She was one of only 17 women to fly a B-17 bomber (the Flying Fortress). During the war she was also a cryptographer, responsible for training decoders all over the country. In 1958, she received the first LPGA Teacher of the Year Award. She was the first woman to design and build a golf course—a nine-hole layout at the Cochran Ranch in Indio, California. She was also the first woman baseball commentator on a coast-to-coast broadcast for the Washington Senators

 Helen Hicks was from Cedarhurst, New York. She won the 1931 U.S. Women's Amateur and turned pro shortly after playing on America's winning 1932 Curtis Cup team. She joined Wilson in 1934 and was the first woman to promote golf equipment by giving clinics. When she turned professional she was called a businesswoman golfer because professional status made women outsiders, traitors to the purity of the sport. From the early 1940s, Helen was actively involved in all aspects of golf—from competing to teaching to writing books. She is a member of the Long Beach Golf Hall of

Fame, the Women's Sports Foundation International Hall of Fame, and the California Golf Hall of Fame.

 Opal Hill came from Kansas City, Missouri. She had a nursing degree and didn't start playing until she was 40 years old. After conquering a life-threatening illness—having been told she only had three years to live—she went on to become a tournament champion. In 1935, she chaired the USGA Women's Committee and is enshrined in the Missouri Sports Hall of Fame. Opal had a motto: "If you lose your health, you may lose your wealth, but if you lose your courage you have lost everything. Courage is the prime requisite of a champion golfer or otherwise."

 Betty Jameson, from Norman, Oklahoma, was a two-time U.S. Amateur champion. When she won the 1947 U.S. Women's Open with a 295 total she became the first woman to break 300 in a major championship. Betty was a great competitor and art lover. She won the 1942 Western Open, a major championship at the time. Since there were very few tournaments during World War II she worked on the *Dallas Times Herald* copy desk. In 1952, she created an LPGA award that honors the person with the lowest scoring average and named it after amateur great Glenna Collette Vare (Patty Berg was the first

Vare Trophy winner). Betty Jameson was one of the six inaugural inductees into the LPGA Tour Hall of Fame.

 Sally Sessions was low amateur in the 1947 U.S. Women's Open finishing second to Betty Jameson. She accomplished the rare feat of winning the City of Muskegon, Michigan tennis and golf championships *on the same day*. She turned professional after winning the 1947 Mexican Women's Open and subsequently joined the Wilson staff. She was an accomplished musician and wrote operas, mostly for local production. She also taught in the Detroit public school system. She died at age 43 from leukemia.

 Marilynn Smith (that's me and I don't want to tell you too much because I want you to read the whole book). I was a 20 year-old University of Kansas college sophomore from Wichita and couldn't believe my newfound life, I was a professional golfer.

 Shirley Spork caddied in Detroit, her hometown. She and I traveled together the first year on tour. Then she became head pro at Ukiah Country Club in California. She was a talented golfer, an even better instructor— twice voted the LPGA National Teacher of the Year. The *New York Times* recognized her abilities this way, *"If there were an LPGA*

Mount Rushmore, Spork and her fellow founder Smith would be chiseled on it." (I'm not sure who the Smith person might be.) Shirley helped establish the LPGA Teaching Division and served as chairperson for six years. She was named LPGA National Teacher of the Year, twice.

 Louise Suggs, from Atlanta, Georgia, turned professional in 1948. You should have seen her play in the wind—she had uncanny success. Ben Hogan said, "If I were to single out one woman in the world today as a model for any other woman aspiring to ideal golf form, it would be Miss Suggs." Her methodical, rhythmic swing served her well under any conditions. Bob Hope called her "Miss Sluggs." She started playing at age 10 under her dad's watchful eye. He was a head pro in Carrollton, Georgia. He was also a former baseball player and manager. During the 1950 Sunset Hills Open, all the caddies were taught to retrieve practice shots on the range with baseball gloves. Louise won 58 tournaments and eight majors. She had an exceptional business mind that we put to good use. She was the LPGA president in 1955, 1956 and 1957 and the first woman inducted into the Georgia Athletic Hall of Fame. Louise was one of the six inaugural inductees into the LPGA Tour Hall of Fame. In 1957, she became the first player to achieve the career grand slam.

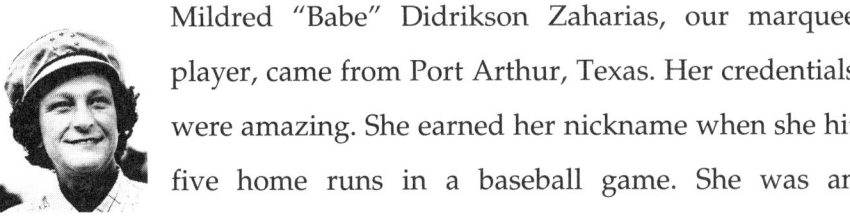 Mildred "Babe" Didrikson Zaharias, our marquee player, came from Port Arthur, Texas. Her credentials were amazing. She earned her nickname when she hit five home runs in a baseball game. She was an Olympic gold medal winner in track and field, and a high school All-American in basketball. The Olympics made her a giant in the sports world and it carried over to the golf course where fans flocked to our tournaments to see the world's best-known female athlete hit phenomenal drives. They showed up for the WOW effect, not to acknowledge tap-in putts with polite fingertip applause.

In 1950, the LPGA had three major championships and Babe was the first player in women's professional golf to win them all. She was quick with a quip. Once before hitting a shot she said, "I'm going to loosen my girdle and let it fly!" The crowd roared. She was an obvious gallery favorite.

Betsy Rawls assessed things this way, "If it hadn't been for the Babe, the LPGA probably wouldn't have existed for at least another ten years. She gave the organization immediate credibility and brought people out to watch."

One of the pleasures of writing this book is being able to view things from a "we lived happily ever after" perspective. At first, we took what we could get—we hit approach shots off hardpan, plucked weeds from our line on putting surfaces. We were grateful to have a place to play so we didn't stop to wonder, "Isn't anybody around here interested in gardening?"

We were a mixture of war heroes, young kids, mothers and well-educated world-class athletes. We did things for ourselves—without management companies, a headquarters staff or swing gurus.

Amazingly, we survived without a corporate logo on our clothing.

All we wanted to do was play golf, and we were determined to make a living doing it.

Ready to Roll

There were only 13 LPGA events on the schedule in 1950, but Spalding kept me busy conducting golf clinics and playing exhibitions throughout the country. I traveled so much you would have thought I was on the lam.

The LPGA had expansion plans for the following year—at least 15 tournaments, $3,000 minimum purses for 36- and 54-hole medal play tournaments and $5,000 purses for 72-hole events. The first guaranteed tournament was at Ponte Vedra, Florida in 1951.

We retained official WPGA events such as the Tampa, Texas and Western Women's National Opens, plus the prestigious Titleholders. Fred Corcoran added a few west coast sponsors. But the biggest addition was the Weathervane Series.

Alvin Handmacher, a clothier famous for Weathervane women's suits, made an offer we couldn't resist. "How about a progressive transcontinental tournament?" he asked. "Tee off in California and hole-out in New York." He said it would be "like a progressive dinner." Well, he was addressing starving athletes. We jumped at the chance. In essence, it would be a *tour within a tour*. We played four 36-hole events each year—in various parts of the country—from 1950 through 1953. He called it the Weathervane

Cross-Country Tournament. Each purse was $15,000, plus a $5,000 bonus for the overall winner. Babe Zaharias, Patty Berg, Betsy Rawls and Louise Suggs earned the bonus in 1950, '51, '52 and '53.

Handmacher gave us the boost we needed.

•

From: Fred Corcoran   *FOR   RELEASE*
Ladies Professional Golf Association   *February 24, 1950*

WEATHERVANE OPEN GOLF CHAMPIONSHIP

Women's golf in this country, which has come quite a way since Mrs. C.S. Brown too the first national tournament in 1895 with a snappy 132 for 18 holes, will really graduate into the big time this spring. Led by the Big Four of women's professional golf: Patty Berg, Betty Jameson, Louise Suggs and Babe Didrickson Zaharias, the girls will be shooting at a total of $17,000 in prize money in the first cross-country tournament ever staged, the first annual Weathervane Open.

The Weathervane Open will consist of four separate 36-hole competitions played on consecutive weekends in four different states: California, Illinois, Ohio and New York. The first competition for the crack pros, as well as the top amateurs in the country, will be staged at the renowned Pebble Beach Golf Course on California's Monterey Peninsula on April 29-30. The following weekend, May 6-7, the girls will be playing Chicago's Skycrest Course, Babe Zaharias' home club. The third competition is scheduled for May 13-14 at the Ridgewood Golf Club in Cleveland, with the windup set for Knollwood Country Club, White Plains, New York, on May 20-21.

In each of the four tournaments, the girls will be shooting at $3,000 in prize money, and the golfer compiling the lowest total for the 144-hole

26

marathon will receive an additional $5,000 and the Weathervane Trophy, donated by Alvin Handmacher.

All proceeds from the tournaments will go to local charities.

The quality of the golf the girls are now producing can best be gauged by Louise Suggs' total of 291 in winning the 1949 National Women's Open and Babe Zaharias' phenomenal 70 in the wind during the 1949 Eastern Open.

•

Alvin Handmacher also sponsored a European swing for players with low cumulative scores in the series. A match was arranged in 1951 at Wentworth, England between the Weathervane Team of Babe, Patty Berg, Peggy Kirk Bell, Betty Bush and Betty Jameson and several men—former British Walker Cup team members. The ladies insisted on playing from the same tees as the men but lost the morning best-ball matches. Patty gathered the girls and laid down the law. "All those who are going to win their matches this afternoon, follow me!" It worked. The women swept the singles matches 6-2. They beat the men.

Betsy Rawls was amazed. "We beat Great Britain's Curtis Cup team in every match," she said. "And after trailing in the foursome matches against a men's team that included a lot of Walker Cup players—from the men's tees—we swept them in the singles matches." The matches drew media coverage from the time the

LPGA players sailed to England until they arrived back in New York a month later.

The international competition only lasted one year. There wouldn't be another transatlantic competition for 39 years when the Solheim Cup came into existence in 1990.

When Betty Hicks returned to the LPGA in 1952, the tour was much improved. The Association still relied on amateurs to fill out tournament fields, and tour players still made more money from exhibitions and clinics than from prize money, but the tournament schedule had more than doubled from the WPGA days and the purses were much larger.

My play in those years wasn't very impressive I lacked confidence. Remember, my choice to turn pro was only supported by my father, Spalding, my pro Mike Murra and a few friends. I didn't even feel worthy of my position on the Spalding staff. As I matured, I felt compelled to win to justify my association and benefits with Spalding.

Fortunately, Fay Crocker believed in me—she would soon be the U.S. Women's Open champion—and she encouraged me to play one shot at a time. She told me to believe in my ability and convinced me that success was achievable. In 1954, I won the Fort

Wayne Open, my first LPGA title. Her support was the 15th club in my bag.

Fred Corcoran was great at lining up tournaments until he resigned in 1953, when the Golf Manufacturers Association abruptly withdrew its financial support and, with it, his paycheck.

Although the LPGA had built up a financial cushion in the first four years, we lacked adequate funds to pay Corcoran's $15,000 salary and couldn't afford to hire a new tournament director. So we searched within for a replacement.

Babe Zaharias took over as tournament director but lasted just two months. Betty Hicks replaced her—playfully suggesting she got the job because she was the only professional with an electric typewriter.

Betsy Rawls felt Betty was an ideal choice, for many reasons. "Betty was a very bright, creative person," she said. "She did a very good job for us."

Betsy was right. Betty Hicks wrote a best selling cookbook and taught aviation after she retired from competitive golf.

In 1955, Fay Crocker and I shared tournament director duties. We made progress, adding more events and prize money, but we realized that acting as tournament director or serving in other official capacities was too much of a load. It consumed us and affected our golf—we weren't playing up to our ability. We spent most of our time planning, promoting and traveling.

The responsibilities seemed endless. We had a Tournament Committee that set up the courses before events. A Pairings Committee prepared the schedule. The treasurer took care of tournament finances and wrote checks to the money winners. After each tournament, a designated player called in the scores to the Associated Press before we left town. And that doesn't take into account all the promotional work. We didn't know what 'delegate' meant. Delegate?

The players were competitive when it came to golf, but off the course we were family. We got along; looked out for each other. To give you an idea, we willingly contributed ten percent of our prize money to the LPGA treasury to ensure its success.

Getting from tournament to tournament was difficult. We traveled by car; doubling up to share expenses. Who could afford to fly? I remember driving 1,600 miles from Spokane, Washington to Waterloo, Iowa in two days.

We traveled caravan style—a string of cars loaded with clubs, shoes, clothes and players. If a car broke down—and it happened now and then—we helped the ones in need. The lead car had three Ping-Pong paddles that we'd hold out the window to communicate while we were driving. The paddles said FOOD, GAS and POTTY so we always knew why we were stopping.

Looking back, it occurs to me that we were at the mercy of the gals in the first car—if they didn't go potty, nobody went potty.

For several months, Shirley Spork and I traveled to events, clinics and promotional activities in my car. I always abided by my father's rule not to exceed the speed limit. When Shirley drove she put tape over the speedometer so "Marilynn won't know when I'm exceeding Daddy's limit."

On long drives we liked to stop at a park, get the gloves out and play catch for a few minutes. Then we'd head off to our destination.

Needless to say, if we were near St. Louis, and the Cardinals were in town, we went to a game

After a one- or two-day trip, we arrived at the new tournament site with a duty list: Laundry, hair dresser, Swing Clinic, course setup, sponsor parties, press commitments, plus the need to practice before the tournament. When you take it all into account, our scores were remarkable. So was our endurance.

31

There were no fitness centers back then. Need more exercise? Hit more golf balls. Betsy Rawls, a Phi Beta Kappa physics graduate from the University of Texas, practiced continually. She had a terrific short game. More than that, she excelled at course management—she really knew how to think her way around a golf course. She learned the game under Harvey Penick's watchful eyes.

We played the pro-am and a 72-hole event from men's tees that measured 6,200 – 6,950 yards. Some courses were finely groomed; others poorly maintained. I remember playing a course in Oklahoma after a drought that had cracks in the ground—none that led to a green, unfortunately. Betty Dodd hit a drive that must have gone 350 yards. It was like driving a golf ball down an airport runway.

One time we went to a ballgame with Babe Zaharias. Babe had a bag of popcorn. She said, "Watch this" as she tossed popcorn in the air and caught it in her mouth. We all tried … and tried … and tried. We were up to our ankles in popcorn before I finally caught a piece in my mouth. She said, "Listen kid, once you do it, don't try it again." Shirley thought that was so profound. She never forgot it.

The 1949 Women's Western Open was played at the Skycrest Country Club in Chicago where Babe Zaharias was the head pro. Before the first round, Babe and George Zaharias were having breakfast with Shirley. Babe asked why Shirley hadn't turned pro. Shirley said she didn't know how. Babe got up, walked over to Shirley, tapped her on the head and said: "Now you're a pro." All Shirley had to do was go to the first tee and register as a pro. Babe was a miracle worker.

During the World Championship at Tam O'Shanter Country Club in Chicago, I was paired with Babe and Patty Berg. We teed off on No. 1 and Babe put her arm around me as we walked off the tee. "Smitty," she said with a straight face, "I love to be paired with you because you always get a gallery." Crowds came out to watch "the Babe" but she wanted to make me feel at ease.

Her sports career gave new meaning to what a female athlete could accomplish. She was a threat every time she competed. Babe was Babe, bigger than life and always 'on stage.' One time she told the press she shot 69 in a practice round when she really shot 73. When asked about it she said, "That's what the press and people want to hear." In the early days we wore skirts—long ones, down to our calves. On impulse, she'd leap hedges like a horse. No one could predict what she'd do next. That merely added to the excitement.

Babe was only 45 when she died of cancer in September 1956. She had been ill since early '53, but recuperated enough to play excellent golf. A year after a colostomy, when some might have expected her to be a shadow of herself, she won the Women's Open by 12 strokes. When she passed away the LPGA faced a public relations problem. Babe was our drawing card. With Babe, we had a sports page story. Without her, would we slide back to agate type in tournament statistics? Would galleries shrink? Golf doesn't require teamwork. But the business of golf does. We were a resilient group, a stubborn group. We met it head on. The LPGA wasn't about to ask for strokes.

"That was a sad day for us," Patty Berg said. "She was a marvelous golfer and a marvelous lady who had done so much for us. She still is tremendously missed today, but it was a team effort. There were many, many champions along with Babe and there are many, many more coming."

She was right. Patty Berg, Betty Jameson, Betsy Rawls and Louise Suggs, the decade's other major winners were still big stars. We had credibility. And four new super stars were about to emerge: Mickey Wright, Kathy Whitworth, Carol Mann and Sandra Haynie.

We Couldn't Have Done Without Them

In the LPGA's formative years, many people, towns and organizations helped promote our tour. In show biz they call them angels. These are some that come to mind.

Joe Albi and his Spokane Athletic Round Table group who helped establish the first Women's Open in 1946.

Alvin Handmacher, the clothier famous for Weathervane women's suits—who I mentioned in detail previously— meant the world to us.

Helen Lengfeld, a well-known California golfer and tournament organizer, scheduled tournaments for us in the early 1950s. She really kept our tour alive with 36-hole events played on excellent courses, including Pebble Beach. Helen was chairperson of United Voluntary Services, a northern California non-profit volunteer organization that worked with veteran's hospitals. She also helped build nine-hole golf courses at Veteran's Hospitals throughout the United States. Helen edited and published *The Golfer* magazine. It later became known as the *National Golfer*.

The Serbin Clothing Company staged an event in Miami for a few years and donated the Serbin Trophy for most points earned by a player during the year.

The Grossinger family, tremendous LPGA supporters from New York, held grand tournaments at their resort in the Catskills.

Jack E. McAuliffe, and his company, The Triangle Conduit and Cable Company, sponsored the Triangle Round-Robin in Massachusetts. They also established the J.E. McAuliffe Memorial.

Waco and Opie Turner staged the Opie Open in Burneyville, Oklahoma at the Turner Lodge and Country Club. In addition to a regular purse, they offered bonus money for every ace, eagle, birdie or par.

Janet Olson from Chicago, offered a $1,000 Hole-In-One Award to any player who made an ace in an LPGA event.

George S. May's Tam O'Shanter and All American and World Tournaments in Chicago gave us a big boost. He was the one who began big money tournament golf. Still, the LPGA share was a mere fraction of the PGA purse.

Harry Root, Maynard Ramsey and Sam Davis worked diligently to start the $3,000 Tampa, Florida Open in 1947. It was our first winter event and we played it for many years.

The Western Golf Association came aboard following the Titleholders, as did the fine folks at the Texas Open.

David Foster, president of the Colgate Company contacted the LPGA and arranged for the first Colgate Dinah Shore tournament.

Several amateurs played in our tournaments. All were accomplished, competitive, wonderful people. It is important to recognize them:

My friend Edean Ihlanfeldt from Seattle won the Canadian Women's Open, was low amateur at the Weathervane event in Seattle, and won the U.S. Senior Women's Amateur Championship. We had a lot in common—she, too, was a baseball player. In fact she had a hard time choosing between baseball, football—yes, football––and golf. At one point, she broke her little finger playing baseball but still went on to win a golf tournament with the finger in a splint.

I also want to recognize Mary Ann Downey, former Maryland Amateur Champion, Grace DeMoss from Oregon; Polly Riley from Ft. Worth; Jean Hopkins from Cleveland; Marge Burns from North Carolina and Patricia Grant from San Antonio. Marge and Shirley Lindsey, who were sisters, came from Illinois and Grace Lenczyk was from Connecticut.

Many amateurs made up the Titleholders field: Anne Quast, Barbara McIntire, Tish Preuss, Carol Diringer, Pat O'Sullivan, Mary Agnes Wall, Dot Kielty and Dot Kirby.

These ladies helped fill out the field because we didn't have many pros in the early days. They didn't necessarily travel around the country, but in some cases—the Florida circuit, for instance—they were able to play in more than one tournament.

This book wouldn't be complete without paying tribute to Charlie Mechem, a lawyer and former CEO of Taft Broadcasting in Cincinnati. Charlie took over as LPGA commissioner in 1990— a critical period for the tour. The PGA Senior Tour was reaching its zenith and that made it difficult for our tour to retain sponsors, let alone attract new ones, and player morale had eroded to an all-time low. I've known Charlie for many years. He is a distinguished gentleman who commands respect. He was the perfect choice, exactly what the LPGA needed. When I talked to him recently he said Jack Nicklaus called LPGA President Judy Dickinson and recommended him. Judy and Charlie both belonged to The Loxahatchee Club in Florida where they met and discussed the situation. Afterward, he told Judy he would consider the position if she would remain as president for another year. The first time Charlie met with the players one of the girls asked, "What is our single biggest challenge?" Charlie laid it on the line: "The players have an inferiority complex," he said. Throughout his five-year term as commissioner he stressed a positive attitude and instilled pride. "My proudest moment," he told me, "was when the players grabbed the reins and rose above everything. Their spirit overcame it."

Beating The Drum

Through the 1950s we took advantage of every opportunity to promote our events. We appeared on radio and television shows, spoke at Kiwanis and Rotary luncheons and gave as many press interviews as possible. Reporters never walked away with an empty notepad. When we got to a new town we asked business owners to put posters in their windows to advertise our tournament.

One time I heard a player say, "Nobody understands publicity like Marilynn does." That meant more than a compliment about my golf swing.

There were no gallery ropes, spectators walked along the fairway with us and I liked to talk to the customers. Once in a while a conversation got so good that I'd walk past my ball without noticing. (I'm reminded of a story about a rookie on the men's tour who holed a long putt. On his way to the next tee he saw his name on the leaderboard, for the first time. He marched down the fairway, his head held high—until he realized that he forgot to tee off.) That beats walking past my ball, doesn't it?

My fan-friendly gene never went away. One time, years later, a reporter wrote, *Anytime Marilynn Smith is playing golf, the game is a bundle of laughs as she raps better with the gallery than anybody who ever strode down the fairway on this feminine tour.* He added *Marilynn talked to herself and the gallery all day Sunday.*

A newspaper article, promoting an upcoming Marilynn Smith clinic at Pasco Municipal Golf Course in Washington, says it all:

The clinic, which is free, begins at 10:00 a.m. It could last for some time. "I'll stay there as long as the people want to ask questions," says the personable Smith.

•

Several players took on special projects—we invented ways to get publicity. I hit golf balls from home plate to center field in St. Louis, Cincinnati and Washington, DC before major league games––then grabbed the microphone and said, "OK folks, the LPGA is in town. Come watch the talented ladies play golf." It was a way to encourage baseball fans to come to our tournament. You can imagine what a kick it was to be on a baseball field. Funny thing, though, nobody asked me to hit a line drive or throw a knuckle ball. Oh, well.

•

One time I hit golf balls at Duncan Park in Spartanburg, South Carolina and a newspaper said:

Few name personalities in professional sports would take time off to appear at a baseball game. But Marilynn did. More than 4,000 fans turned out to see her. Even the most hardened bleacherite was warmed by her personality and amazed at her ease as she socked them over the centerfield wall and out of sight. One observer commented: "The government should send her on a world tour. If anyone can make friends for this country, she can."

•

I drove golf balls from, perhaps, the world's largest floating tee: the flight deck of the Navy's newest aircraft carrier, the USS Independence. The ship—docked at the Brooklyn Navy Yard—was 325 yards long—a par-4! The challenge was to drive a ball the length of the ship into the water. As if that wasn't enough, the Navy expected us to do it on the fly. (I say 'us' because, in addition to me, there were three men pros.) Mike Turnesa, at that time a club pro, hit one 235 yards in the air that flew past a couple ensigns on the bow and bounced into the East River. A fore-caddie would have announced, "Out of bounds, and probably lost."

•

A memorable promotion (for me, not so memorable) occurred when Shirley Spork and I went to a boxing match in Landover, Maryland.

We were in the front row watching one boxer pummel the other one. It was dreadful. The guy was getting knocked all over the ring, sweat sprayed everywhere when punches landed and the fighters were splattered with blood. Now, I don't handle those things very well. You couldn't get me in the ring at gunpoint. Thank goodness for Shirley. After the fight, she climbed through the ropes, grabbed the microphone and announced the U.S. Women's Open dates and encouraged the crowd to come see us play. Nobody booed her (that was a good sign). We don't know if she convinced any boxing fans to show up at Prince George's Golf Club … although a guy at a par-3 was perched on a stool he swiped from a gym. Hah.

•

In 1952, several LPGA gals made their screen debut in MGM's movie *Pat and Mike* starring Katharine Hepburn, Spencer Tracy and Aldo Ray. It was the story of a golfer (Hepburn) who competed for the lady's golf championship. Babe Zaharias, Betty Hicks, Helen Dettweiler and Beverly Hanson played themselves, as did tennis stars Don Budge, Alice Marble and Gussie Moran. The reviews said, "Movie buffs flocked to theaters to see the stars plus a long list of athletes." We hoped they would flock to our tournaments, as well.

•

In 1958, *Sports Illustrated* put on a Style Show in Dallas at Glen Lakes Country Club preceding the Civitan Ladies Open. They selected 10 girls to model. We wore high heels, dresses, hats and gloves—a departure from our golf course apparel. I must say we turned a lot of heads. In 1963, we were in another *Sports Illustrated* Style Show, this time in Las Vegas prior to the LPGA Championship at Stardust Country Club. Thankfully, it was before *Sports Illustrated* launched their annual swimsuit issue.

•

There was a "Fun Night" after the dinner at the Titleholders Tournament in Augusta. We entertained the club members and sponsors. Babe played the harmonica, accompanying Betty Dodd who sang in her Elvis-like voice and played the guitar. Jackie Pung took off her shoes and danced a hula. Patty Berg, Shirley Englehorn and I sang. Good grief, we had fun. We were off-key but it didn't stop our rendition of *Five Foot Two, Eyes of Blue* and *I'm Looking Over A Four Leaf Clover*. The audience ate it up. So did we. We got away from pressing to play good golf, if only for an evening. I know it's trite to say, 'Those were the days!' but, you know what? They really were.

One year, the Titleholders Association wanted to honor Louise Suggs for her outstanding career and, in particular, her four

Titleholders victories. A presentation was planned in secrecy, but Louise didn't plan to show up on the night of the event. Behind the scenes arm-twisting got her there, but she didn't appear too happy about it. After dinner and the Fun Night, the "This is your life Louise Suggs" surprise presentation took place. She received the *Golf Digest* award plaque for the best performance average of 1959. "I was flabbergasted," she said afterwards, through teary eyes. "I couldn't believe the award and the messages that came from far and wide"

•

We did our best to create goodwill among our sponsors and the public. We were accessible to the media who said we were the most cooperative of all professional athletes. That was encouraging.

•

At end of the decade, the LPGA not only survived, we nearly doubled the number of events and more than quadrupled prize money. In 1959, we had 26 tournaments and played for $200,000.

•

Marlene Hagge said, "I was so young when I joined the LPGA that I didn't realize the significance, but now I feel a great sense of pride having been involved right from the start. It's hard for young players to understand what it was like in the beginning. Love of golf, love of competition was our motivation, not money because there wasn't any. We always have to keep something in reserve to give back to the Association that has given us the opportunity to play."

Left: I was the pitcher, coach and manager of a boy's baseball team. Right: Without a uniform (no wonder, it snowed that day). Below: My parents, Alma and Lynn Smith—from whom my name Marilynn, is uniquely spelled.

The LPGA was founded in 1950 at Rolling HIll Country Club in Wichita, Kansas, my home town. It was also the last day of the U.S. Women's Open. In 2012, the LPGA commemorated the event with this plaque featuring the founders' pictures.

Babe Zaharias (left) and I were just off the golf course and ready to celebrate the official beginning of our new organization. The man in the background is my dad.

Upper left: Grace Lenczyk (right) and I had fun with Shirley Spork at the 1948 Women's National Intercollegiate Golf Tournament at Ohio State's Scarlet Course.

Upper right: The first time I met Bing Crosby I offered him a cookie from the can in my hand. He declined. I asked again. He said ok. When he took the top off a jack-in-the-box flew out. What was I thinking?

Lower left: Trying to look my best. Low hemlines didn't necessarily mean low scores.

My Spalding publicity photo. Notice the rabbit's foot attached to my belt for good luck.

Signing a new tournament contract in 1958, at the Savoy Hotel in New York. Left to right, standing: Fred Corcoran, LPGA tournament director; Eileen Staub, LPGA promotions manager. Seated: I'm on the left; Frank Hoiles, president of Alliance Country Club in Ohio.

Left: With my dad. Right: Betsy, Jackie and I represented the three equipment manufacturers that paid Fred Corcoran, our first tournament director's, salary.

Below: At a Memphis, Tennessee tournament. Back row (l-r): Barbara Romack, Kathy Whitworth, Murle Breer, Mary Ann Reynolds, Beverly Hanson, Louise Suggs, Peggy Kirk Bell, Mickey Wright. Front row: Jo Ann Prentice, Marlene Bauer Hagge, Gloria Armstrong, Joyce Ziske, Marilynn Smith, Bonnie Randolph.

Above: Spring training in Florida, a day to remember. New York Yankee manager, Casey Stengel, checked the hop on my fastball as a St. Petersburg Times sports reporter looked on.

Below right: Yankee coach, Bill Dickey, played for 17 years and caught in 1,789 games—but it was the first time he saw a skirt on the mound.

Upper left: Clutching the 1964 Titleholders trophy, my second major win. Back-to-back Titleholders championships.

Upper right: Arriving in Australia in 1963 to conduct clinics and exhibitions.

Below left: In Luxembourg with Gene Sarazan in 1964. I was filming a Shell's Wonderful World of Golf match against Marley Spearman, the English Amateur champion.

Above: 1970. Left to right: Marlene Hagge, Alice Bauer, Betsy Rawls, Betty McKinnon, Beverly Hanson, Marilynn Smith and Patty Berg.

Below: 1979. Receiving the first Patty Berg Award, given by the LPGA to an individual who "exemplifies diplomacy, sportsmanship, goodwill and contributions to the game of golf." An extraordinary honor.

The Business Side

In 1956, LPGA President Louise Suggs and I met with a group of Detroit businessmen headed by Blaine Enon, president of Forest Lake Country Club in Bloomfield Hills, near Detroit. It was time to seek outside advice regarding our organizational structure. Blaine used his club's resources, and their guidance put us on the right track. He and his board assured us that it was financially feasible to hire a tournament director and small staff. They even helped conduct the interviews. We hired Bob Renner, a Ft. Wayne sportswriter for $15,000.

The following year, 1957, Louise Suggs, Mary Lena Faulk and I went to Augusta during Masters week to seek PGA of America President Harold Sargent's help. We wanted to expand our tournament schedule. We felt that that adding more women's events would be good for all professional golf, including the men's tour. But we needed help.

True confession: After our meetings, Mary Lena and I made a daily beeline for the practice tee to watch Ben Hogan hit balls. Then we dashed to the hotel and sat in the lobby so we could wave at him when he came in. We had a crush on *Ben Hogan*. (I can't believe I'm telling you this.)

49

Ahem, back to business.

Harold Sargent was willing to assist. The PGA 'loaned' us Ed Carter, their tournament director, for a year to get us going. He took over Bob Renner's duties. The LPGA paid Ed $7,500 and gave him a $1,800 expense allowance. We also paid for an office in San Francisco.

Ed arranged tournaments in small towns that couldn't afford the men's purses—a perfect strategy. We played in Gatlinburg, Tennessee; Ashville, North Carolina; Rockton, Illinois and Santa Barbara, California.

We also asked three women's golf organizations to raise their prize money from our $3,500 minimum to a $5,000 minimum. The Titleholders and the Western Association agreed. The Texas Open declined, so we lost a good tournament. But, in the interest of progress, we had no choice.

Clinics and Exhibitions

Spalding kept me busy conducting clinics and exhibitions during our off weeks. I filed reports afterwards, like this one from 1956. Fay Crocker, also a Spalding staffer, participated.

Details of my clinics and exhibitions in Gene Gleissner's territory:

Fort Riley G C, Ft. Riley, Kansas — 9/23/56

Publicity: Did not arrive in time for use.

Attendance: Approximately 200 persons.

Nine-hole match played with two local women and two men.

Scores: Fay 37, myself 36.

The response to this clinic was exceptionally good, especially since the club pro did the only promotion.

Topeka G C, Topeka, Kansas — 9/24/56

Publicity: Arrived the day of the clinic. However, they did have newspapermen there to cover the exhibition and the following day a nice article and a picture of us appeared in the *Topeka Daily Capital*.

Attendance: Approximately 125 persons.

Nine hole match played with two local ladies.

Scores: Fay 37, myself 39.

Excelsior Springs C C, Excelsior Springs, Missouri — 9/25/56

Publicity: Arrived day before clinic—therefore was of little use.

Attendance: Approximately 25 persons.

Nine hole match played with two local ladies.
Scores: Fay 37, myself 35.

Red Oak C C, Red Oak, Iowa — 9/26/56

Publicity: Pictures arrived Monday.

Attendance: Approximately 100 persons.

Match played with three local men and Phyllis Germain, pro from Atlantic.

Scores: Fay 37, myself 36.

Carroll C C, Carroll, Iowa — 9/27/56

Publicity: Info sheet arrived a week prior to clinic and pictures on Monday. Picture in paper Wednesday.

Attendance: Approximately 40 persons.

Match played with two local men.

Scores: Fay and I had 37.

Newton C C, Newton, Iowa — 9/28/56

Publicity: Info sheet a week ahead and pictures Tuesday. A reporter was present and pictures were taken before the match.

Attendance: Approximately 50 persons.

Match played with two local girls. Both Fay and I had 37 on a very windy, dusty day, which resulted in poor attendance.

In my opinion, the pros at these clubs do not have the necessary time to satisfactorily promote exhibitions. Would it be possible for the publicity to be sent directly to the sports editors, as well as to the club pro?

Sincerely yours,

Marilynn Smith

Golfing With the Ladies

I wrote this in 1958. Clacked it out on a typewriter. It says a lot about tour life, and our efforts to reach out to the public.

GOLFING WITH THE LADIES' P.G.A.

By Marilynn Smith,

A. G. Spalding & Bros., Inc., Golf Consultant and President, Ladies' Professional Golf Association

Have clubs, will travel. This could well be the motto of the Ladies' Professional Golf Association. From January through October the tournament members of the L.P.G.A. continuously crisscross the highways and byways of the U.S.A. as they trek their way from tournament site to tournament site. Winter in Florida, Spring and Summer in Georgia, South Carolina, Texas, Virginia, New York, Michigan, Pennsylvania and Illinois. Fall in Nevada and California.

Throughout this exciting, nomadic existence the girls swing their mighty clubs in quest of fame and fortune.

The LPGA, a non-profit organization, has 59 members, 25 of whom play the entire golf circuit. Between 25 and 30 tournaments are scheduled each year with prize money totaling about $160,000. The organization is growing very rapidly and it is expected that the 1958 season will have prize money in excess of $200,000.

The outwardly glamorous appearance of the tournament trail is slightly hampered when it becomes apparent that hard work and skill are the prime requirements if a touring pro is to make ends meet, let alone make a profit at the end of 40,000 wearying miles of travel a year. Let's, for example, illustrate a typical day in the life of a touring golf professional. She arises early and after a hearty breakfast, drives out to the golf course for an hour or two of practice prior to tee-off time. Eighteen holes of concentrated play will follow, and if a certain shot requires special attention at the end of the day's play she will wend her way back to the practice tee for another workout. Later, a possible TV appearance, dinner with tournament officials, then back to the motel to engage in letter writing, expense accounts, ironing, laundry and shoe polishing, winding up an exhausting 15 hours. This readily shows the physical stamina required by the girls who make this their life work.

Have clubs, will travel? Yes, because the tournament pros agree that these hardships are minor compared with the pleasure derived from meeting wonderful people and the joys of traveling throughout this hospitable and magnificent country. The thrill of competition and the knowledge that the

LPGA is helping, in many ways, to bring the great game of golf to thousands of fans helps make this an exciting and satisfying career.

Many non-tournament playing members, we are proud to say, through their teaching and guidance, assist the young people of America. It is mainly through their efforts that golf is brought into high schools and colleges, thus affording the young people an opportunity to benefit from this sport at an early age.

Other members have teaching positions at various country clubs and municipal golf courses and are, through their efforts, adding impetus to participation of women in golf. It is hoped that more and more opportunities as golf instructors will be available to women professionals as they make fine teachers with their patience, knowledge and ability. As can be readily seen, it is not only the tournament golfing professional who benefits from a golfing career. The LPGA hopes that in the near future more and more young women will join its ranks and thus help to make the organization a stronger and more vital force in the sports world.

Would you like to have a touring LPGA member give a golf demonstration at your school? If so, either communicate with the secretary of the LPGA, 2100 Jones St., San Francisco, California, giving the name of the pro you would like to have visit your school, or write to any of the manufacturers of golf equipment who have any LPGA members or golf consultants on their staff. Such an exhibition could prove very interesting and beneficial to all schools of golf.

Chief Executive

By the time I took over as president in 1958 we had gained visibility. In the beginning we were mostly unknowns from hither and yon who clustered in search of a place—any place—to play a tournament, sometimes in virtual privacy for what amounted to chicken feed. We were way past all that.

The next logical step: Develop a more marketable image and emphasize it. We can play; let's look good doing it. I had been told that people remembered me more for my color-coordinated outfits, earrings and ever-present pearl necklace than for any particular shot or tournament. So I felt comfortable when I stressed that personal appearance had to be a priority.

The executive board supported me. Together, we encouraged our members to be concerned about the way they presented themselves. Galleries and potential sponsors expected to see attractive women on the course; we were happy to oblige.

The executive board consisted of Bonnie Randolph, vice president Mary Lena Faulk, treasurer Mary Ann Reynolds, secretary Betsy Rawls, member-at large Beverly Hanson. They, among others, were instrumental in helping us accomplish our goals. They were intelligent and creative and, most importantly, courageous. Case in point: Betsy Rawls has since been named one of the most influential women in golf.

There were other achievements, as well, more tangible ones. We launched innovative programs and had several major developments.

In 1958, we brought Fred Corcoran back as tournament director and hired Joe McDonald as Corcoran's on-tour assistant.

Eileen Stulb, who owned an advertising agency in Augusta, was hired to handle the LPGA's publicity while the players continued to manage tournament operations. Eileen was an expert when it came to women's golf. She was an outstanding amateur player and a member of the Georgia Golf Hall of Fame. She worked with us until 1962. When she left we hired Nan Berry Ryan as director of public relations. Nan had been assistant public relations director for the PGA, and senior editor of the PGA magazine.

Everybody rolled up their sleeves and made things happen. We didn't look at the work or the hours involved as a sacrifice. We did it because we were doing something for a lot of good people.

In 1958, we established the Teacher of the Year Award. It honors the lady teaching professional who most exemplifies her profession. Helen Dettweiler was the first winner. After more than a half-century, the award continues to be coveted by our Teaching Division professionals—it honors the best of the best.

In 1958, we played a distinctive 90-hole event: the Triangle Round Robin at Tedesco Country Club in Marblehead, Massachusetts. We played in a different foursome in every round and made or lost points by comparing our stroke score with the others in the foursome. We received a point for every stroke better than another member of the foursome, and lost a point for every stroke higher. Louise Suggs' +51 score won first place and $1,425.

I was reelected at the LPGA Annual Meeting in Burneyville, Oklahoma. Marlene Hagge was elected vice president, Mary Lena Faulk, treasurer and Mickey Wright, secretary.

We, along with Louise Suggs, member-at-large, made up the 1959 LPGA Executive Board.

Committee assignments:

Tournament Committee: Betsy Rawls, chairman; Kathy Cornelius and Marlene Hagge.

Pairings Committee: Wanda Sanches, Jon Snyder, Jackie Pung and Jo Ann Prentice.

Membership Committee: Ruth Jessen, Bonnie Randolph and Jackie Pung.

Publicity Chairman: Beverly Hanson.

Clinic Committee: Patty Berg and Beverly Hanson; Assistants: Sybil Griffin and Pat Devany.

Statistician: Joyce Ziske; Assistant: Murle MacKenzie.

•

In 1959, we started to play a pro-am the day before tournaments, teaming the girls with local amateurs in best-ball foursomes. By 1965, a pro-am was part of almost every tour stop. A day of golf and the accompanying cocktail party gave the girls an opportunity to meet the patrons and express their appreciation. And it worked both ways. The patrons and sponsors got to know the players, firsthand, in a relaxed setting. Word spread. The participants told friends and neighbors about their experience. The following year an even larger slice of the community looked forward to the girls returning.

The LPGA Teaching Division—renamed the LPGA Teaching and Club Professional (T&CP) Division—was founded in 1959. Shirley Spork and I were determined to get it established. We tried to start the program several years earlier but it was a tough sell; understandably, voted down. The organization had been struggling to survive, scrambling to find new tournaments and the timing wasn't right. But we submitted it to the membership again in 1959 and it passed—by a one-vote margin.

We'll never know who cast the deciding vote, but she should be celebrated because the T&CP has enjoyed unprecedented growth thanks to its dedication to teaching and instruction, business management, and high school and college team coaching. The T&CP administers the Association's grassroots programs for youth and women, in addition to teaching the game to men, women and children across the country.

There are more than 1,400 members today. And today's curriculum reflects the same general objectives set out by the founders in 1959. That's remarkable.

Shirley Spork summed it up this way, "We weren't thinking about creating something special. Just doing what we thought was correct. People aught to be given the opportunity to be taught with a sincere method. The purpose was to gain members, bring people to the game and standardize teaching methods. We wanted to locate the best teachers and have them present their ideas."

Betty Hicks, the first chairwoman, remembered that, at the time, if someone—most likely a man—was a good player, they would teach their own particular game using their personal style, based on their own experiences. "You could either take it or leave it," she said. "It became apparent that there was no place for teachers to get training and we needed people who were interested in teaching teachers how to teach. Some are born with the ability to teach, but that certainly wasn't the case with every one. That's why we had to help."

In 1960, we held the first LPGA National Golf Schools. There were six: two at the University of Michigan in Ann Arbor, two at the University of North Carolina in Greensboro, one at the University of Vermont in Burlington and one at Bowling Green State University in Bowling Green, Ohio.

Most attendees were college coaches anxious to learn how to teach golf. Participants paid their own expenses. Shirley Spork, Barbara Rotvig, Ellen Griffin and I made up the faculty.

In 1961, Shirley and Barbara Rotvig co-chaired the School. Its prominence grew year by year and, in time, the LPGA was able to pay the School's operational expenses.

Dr. Betsy Clark, an education consultant for the National Golf Foundation who joined the LPGA Teaching Division in 1980, was appointed education coordinator in 1986 and began working with the LPGA teacher education program.

"Basic golf knowledge alone is not enough to be an effective teacher of the game," she said. "We have to look at the way the student learns and then decide how best to communicate knowledge in the acquisition of skill to the student."

She continued, "Currently, we are the only association in the golf industry that offers a comprehensive teacher certification program, and the LPGA T&CP Division is recognized as a leader in teacher training."

Low scores draw large crowds. So, in 1960, we moved the tees forward, to the front of the regular men's tees, and played courses that measured 6,200 – 6,400 yards. We saw immediate results and attendance increased. (In the early years, Babe Zaharias insisted on playing longer courses that gave her an advantage, or she'd threaten to withdraw. Organizers relented, fearing fewer ticket sales.)

Four-day events plus a pro-am meant five days of golf and left little time for travel and promotion. In 1963 we changed most events to 54-holes plus a pro-am.

Patty Berg emceed clinics at tournament sites to raise money for the treasury. She had a great sense of humor, did a comedy routine and kept the audience entertained. Once in a while, I was the emcee. We dubbed the clinics the LPGA Swing Parade and charged sponsors $300. The fact that touring pros with star power were involved helped draw a crowd. There was little electronic media instruction in those days, so folks had a chance to see the best in the game demonstrate different shots. The emcee introduced a player— perhaps Marlene Hagge or Barbara Romack, both great short-iron players; or Shirley Englehorn, who hit amazing one-iron shots. The player would hit shots while we described the different ways to play the particular club, when to use it depending on lie, distance and course conditions, etc. We demonstrated irons and woods, answered questions and did our best to make the session enjoyable and instructive.

Occasionally, Shirley Spork wore an Emmett Kelly clown costume and entertained the Swing Parade crowd by hitting trick shots. It got everybody's attention and made the subsequent learning experience fun.

One afternoon, when I emceed a clinic, Wiffi Smith was a participant and I introduced her this way: "Miss Margaret 'Wiffi' Smith will show you how to hit a two-iron." I held my arm out gesturing toward her, but she wasn't there. "OK, Wiffi, where are you?" I shouted. At that instant she galloped to the tee astride a quarter horse. She dismounted, pounded a few two-irons, jumped back on the horse and rode off into the sunset. Yes, there really was a sunset. It was late.

The President's Report

At the end of my three-year term, I submitted this report to the members:

President's Report to Membership – September 26, 1960.

Ladies' PGA San Antonio, Texas

This year it was heartwarming to see so many of our members striving successfully for better sponsor relations. Our dress and manner have improved tremendously and it is my hope that the importance of this phase of our public relations will be uppermost in our minds.

This year has seen a slight recession in our total prize money over last year, but this still ranks as our second best financial year. In 1959 our purses totaled $213,000.00 with 26 tournaments and 3 Pro-Ams. This year we played for $198,700.00, in 24 tournaments and 2 Pro-Ams. I would like to bring to your attention that five tournaments totaling over $49,000.00 were not on our schedule this year because of the following reasons:

1. Mt. Prospect $16,000 – it was felt that this type of sponsor was not one which the LPGA would be wise in cultivating and late developments have proved that we were correct.

2. Sanford, Fla. $6,000 – The N.Y. Giants were in a process of selling their establishment in Florida.

3. Kansas City, Mo. $7,500 – Due to an unfortunate accident where a number of spectators were injured by a runaway electric cart during the men's PGA event and to the

fact that a lawsuit was involved the K.C. Golf Assoc. felt it wise not to schedule our event at that time.

4. Jacksonville, Fla. $6,500 – Integration closed all Municipal golf courses and sponsors were unable to find a new host course.

5. Burneyville, Okla. $13,000 plus - Waco and Opie Turner did not sponsor the tournament this year for various reasons. Tournament could not be written off income tax and Opie's poor health.

It is easy to note that our organization was the victim of circumstances and that the 1960 tour did not merit severe criticism of a defeatist nature.

After 3 years of experience as President I have come to the conclusion that the complexities and magnitude of the job facing the President and her Executive Board are so great and with our steady growth these yearly become greater, that every member of the organization must realize that constructive criticism is very healthy but that negative thoughts only help to undermine the morale of the women who are generously giving their valuable time and effort in an honorary capacity to making our organization bigger and better. It is up to each and every one of us to realize that this is a business and that we are all women in business. We are lucky that we are partners in a business, not just mere employees. As such we have a direct interest in expanding, and we should, at all times, be more than willing to graciously cooperate to the fullest extent of our capabilities to make our business a great success. A player who as President has to combine the aptitudes of liaison officer, tournament director, office girl, social hostess, telephone operator, all highly specialized jobs, is in no position to give 100% to any one of them. To eliminate part of this tremendous responsibility it was decided at a meeting in Worcester, Mass., with Fred Corcoran and the Executive Board to hire Mr. Joe McDonald, highly recommended by Fred Corcoran, to act as our Tournament

Coordinator and Liaison Officer. Thus we maintain our New York office with Fred as our Tournament Director and Joe as his and our representative in the field. It is my sincere hope that this program will considerably lighten the task of the next President and Executive Board. Eileen Stulb will continue as our Promotion Director. I would like to stress the outstanding job that she and her assistants are doing for us. In this respect, I would like to urge everybody to reply to Eileen's inquiries promptly, as she cannot work efficiently without the requested information.

The 1961 tour is scheduled to begin January 13-15 at Sea Island, Ga. Florida dates will be supplied to you as soon as definite commitments are obtained. I have great hopes that 1961 will be the greatest year of our history and that the combination of our staff and our membership in cooperation, will lead this organization to a future that will find it the leading force in women's golf not only in this country, but also in the entire world.

I would like to make the following suggestions:

1. That our Tournament Coordinator makes every effort to obtain a minimum of $8,500 for the 1961 summer tournaments.

2. That we alternate tournament sites and sponsors yearly so that the old saying "familiarity breeds contempt" doesn't hold us back. For example: One year we could begin tour in California in February and work southeastward. The next year we could begin in Florida and work southwestward.

3. That our Tournament Coordinator obtain exhibition matches for girls who do not give clinics for manufacturers. I further suggest that 10% of any money earned by these appearances, be put in the LPGA treasury to help defray expenses.

4. That the LPGA study and organize the possibility of instituting a Golf Course Rating Committee as a professional service to be available to clubs who request assistance in rating their courses for ladies' par. This Professional Service could be advertised in leading golf magazines and might prove of financial benefit to our treasury.

5. That not all members appear in every clinic. Suggest two teams to alternate.

6. That because we are such a small group, and women, it would seem unwise at this time to obtain insurance coverage on the group plan. Each tournament player should carry insurance on an individual basis.

7. That more experienced LPGA members conduct a seminar for tournament players, teaching them how to conduct a clinic and explaining basic fundamentals of the golf swing, so they can better represent LPGA when giving clinics and exhibitions.

8. That the LPGA conduct a rule study at least three times a year in order that each member will be more informed and can therefore, set a higher standard for the game of golf and for our organization.

9. That a ladies' national golf day be set aside similar to Men's National Golf Day. Women only would participate against our LPGA Champion and USGA National Champion. This is to be implemented by our Business Manager.

10. That the LPGA co-sponsor a scotch foursome type tournament with women amateurs as partners. This might be a good Florida event.

11. That a committee be appointed to up-date our constitution.

12. That the prize money distribution be studied for a possible change.

Fred Corcoran and his lawyer, Lee Eastman, are drawing up a new LPGA Sponsor tournament agreement with new stipulations approved by the Executive Board. I would suggest Eileen Stulb furnish each tournament player a copy of the contract in order that each of us may be aware of the responsibilities we have to our sponsor and vice versa.

The LPGA sweaters have been ordered by Bonnie Randolph and should be ready soon. Bonnie will distribute them.

One of the most important contributions to the improvement of women's golf was the LPGA National Golf School held at the U. of Michigan last June. The Teaching Committee with Barbara Rotvig doing most of the organizing arranged the 5-day school. She is to be congratulated and thanked for her great interest and contribution to improving golf knowledge of physical education and recreation teachers. LPGA members devoting time to this school were Shirley Spork, Betty Hicks, Jackie Pung, Mary Ann Reynolds, and Marilynn Smith. The Executive Board has approved a continuation of the Golf School for 1961. I feel that this endeavor will flourish through the years and I urge all LPGA members to assist in any way possible to make it an outstanding success.

Louise Suggs has interested her friend, Bob Hope in producing Ladies' All Star Golf for Television. Fred Corcoran is now working out details with his lawyer. A meeting has been planned for October 13, between Hope and Fred and members of our group. I would suggest a TV Committee be named with Louise Suggs as Chairman, to personally represent our group. Two contracts are now being written by Mr. Eastman and will be approved by this Committee at the Oct. 13, meeting.

Mr. Bill Martin is very interested in televising 2 live shows, which would involve shooting the final round of two of our major events.

A suggestion made by Betty Bush at the French Lick, Ind. meeting last July has been studied. Her idea would be to have the LPGA pay each member a certain amount of money to insure that this member so obligated would faithfully proceed to discharge her duties to the LPGA. Two lawyers in San Antonio said that the only appreciable effect would be psychological and the fact that the member did not live up to her part of the agreement would have no value if court tested. They further stated that our fine system and suspension clause should be sufficient to guarantee the LPGA protection from a member not willing to face her responsibilities.

Due to the fact that our organization is expanding so rapidly it was considered wise by the Executive Board to have our own legal representative. Mr. Owen West, from Chicago, Ill., has graciously consented to act as our attorney in an honorary capacity whenever requested.

I personally wish to thank all the Committees for the help they have given the organization the past year.

It has been a pleasure and a rich experience for me to represent this organization as President the last three years, and you may be assured that I will be available to cooperate to the best of my ability with the new Executive Board. I am confident that this organization presenting a united front at all times will grow to bigger and better achievements.

Many thanks for your help and cooperation.

Respectfully submitted,

Marilynn Smith, President, Ladies' PGA

Teaching Teachers to Teach

The LPGA Teaching and Club Professionals (T&CP) celebrated their 50th anniversary in 2009.

Shirley Spork took over the chairmanship from Betty Hicks in 1960 and served through 1967. It was the period when the National Golf Schools began and grew in popularity. Golf instructors were taught to teach more effectively and prospective golf instructors got off on the right foot using proven teaching methods from day one.

The LPGA T&CP rapidly gained recognition for its standards of acceptance.

In 1966, Ellen Griffin played a lead role in getting the National Golf Foundation (NGF) to partner with the LPGA and join the educational movement. Ellen, Shirley Spork, Lorraine Abbott and many other LPGA and PGA members conducted NGF seminars that helped the NGF expand its consultant staff. The objective was to have 70 top instructors who, in turn, would hold seminars and workshops nationally for 30,000 high school and college golf coaches.

I participated in a weeklong seminar for the NGF consultant staff and candidates for the staff. There were 40 hours of accredited programming, plus hands-on experience working with prominent golf educators. Golf instructors Gary Wiren, Bob Toski, Jim Flick and Bill Strassbaugh were on hand; Bert Yancy and I represented the touring professionals.

Over the years the T&CP has prospered and diversified. It has a written constitution and by-laws. The membership stands at 1,400 and is growing. There are five geographic sections, each with appointed officers.

The best of the best are recognized with annual awards: The LPGA Teacher of the Year, LPGA Professional of the Year, LPGA Coach of the Year and the Ellen Griffin Rolex Award. There is also an annual LPGA T&CP National Championship.

The LPGA T&CP participates in several community outreach programs. The Urban Youth Golf Program, established in 1989 by Sandy La Bauve, connects girls ages 7 to 17 with the game. The LPGA Junior Golf Program outfits kids with shirts, clubs and shoes and provides free access to area golf courses for a six-week lesson series supervised by T&CP and PGA of America members. LPGA Golf Clinics for Women in business to help them become more comfortable with golf as a sport and a business tool. The LPGA participates in The First Tee that gives junior golfers the opportunity to interact with LPGA players and T&CP members at many LPGA tournaments.

All this (and more) came into being in 1959, by a slim one-vote margin.

The 1960s and 1970s

Fred Corcoran left in late 1960 and Lennie Wirtz, a MacGregor salesman and one of the Big Ten's top basketball officials, took over and remained with us for nine years. Lennie had two goals when he came on board: Increase total prize money to $350,000 and see that 20 players meet expenses by earning at least $5,000 apiece. In 1965, 25 players made more than $5,000 and 16 of them made more than $10,000. Tournament purses grew to $509,500 in 1966, but fell to $435,250 the next year because four tournaments were dropped.

It was time for the LPGA to do more to honor its own with annual awards. In 1962, we established the LPGA Rookie of the Year Award—Mary Mills was the first recipient. Back in 1952, Betty Jameson had donated the Vare Trophy.

In 1963, the final round of the U.S. Women's Open was televised. That was significant, but all four rounds wouldn't be televised until the Nabisco-Dinah Shore in 1982.

Althea Gibson, the famous tennis player, became the first African American woman to play on the LPGA tour in 1964. We were scheduled to play a tournament in Texas, but the management wouldn't let her enter the clubhouse. Collectively, Lennie Wirtz and all the players agreed to move it to another location where she would be accepted and welcome to enjoy the amenities. I'm pleased that the LPGA has always been open to players of any color. Althea was a fine person and a superior role model for the LPGA. Her golf career only spanned a few years.

The qualifications to play the tour were demanding. A rookie had to beat 20 percent of the professional field in three out of four consecutive tournaments to earn a card. There was a $50 entry fee until they were accepted. Then they played without a fee.

In 1966, Kathy Whitworth won the first LPGA Player of the Year Award—and went on to win it seven of the first eight years.

The LPGA Tour Hall of Fame was established in 1967. The first inductees were Patty Berg, Betty Jameson, Louise Suggs, Betsy Rawls, Babe Zaharias and Mickey Wright.

Carol Mann's first victory was the 1964 Women's Western Open and she went on to win ten times in 1968 and eight times in 1969.

By 1969, our schedule had 24 tournaments with $600,000 in total prize money.

Kathy Whitworth was the LPGA's leading money winner in 1970, earning $30,235. Women lagged behind men in prize money and recognition, but interest was picking up. Kathy joined the tour in 1959, and could have considered another way to make a living—her stroke average for the year was 80.30. It looked like a typo. Skeptics thought she didn't have what it takes, but she was chasing a dream and refused to quit. What grit. She won 88 tournaments and remains golf's all-time career winner. Mickey Wright and Sam Snead won 82 times, Tiger Woods 74, Jack Nicklaus 73 and Annika Sorenstam 72.

An explosion of popular champions dominated the 1970s. JoAnne Carner, Judy Rankin, Donna Caponi, Jan Stephenson, Amy Alcott, Jane Blalock and Susie Maxwell Berning captured headlines and fueled growth. Tournaments often concluded with one of them clutching the winner's trophy.

In 1971, large corporations began to invest in the LPGA tour. Comparatively speaking, our rates were a bargain. Sears, Sealy, Mazda, Suzuki, Pepsi and Eve cigarettes sponsored tournaments.

It was time for the LPGA to name its first commissioner. Ray Volpe, a marketing expert, came onboard in 1975. He took the job because he believed we had talent, personalities and charisma. He set out to sell women's golf to the right people—sponsors, big-money sponsors—and he succeeded. He knew it was a mistake for anyone to even consider the women versus men angle (although a mixed tournament displaying cooperation between the tours was successful). He promoted our players as the best women golfers in the world. Under his leadership the LPGA became a significant business entity in the sports world. Volpe established a retirement plan for the players, the first ever for a non-team sport. In 1980, there was a stipulation that you had to play in ten tournaments to qualify. I only played in nine. In fact, twenty players played in fewer than ten tournaments, but we weren't notified about the stipulation. The LPGA recognized the mistake and those players were paid $5,000.

In 1976, Judy Rankin became the first player to earn more than $100,000. All those zeros sure looked good.

In late 1977, Nancy Lopez arrived. Did she ever. She was an immediate star, but her dynamic career was really launched in 1978, her first full year on tour when she won nine times including five victories in a row. She was Player of the Year, Rookie of the Year, and won the Vare Trophy for lowest scoring average.

Nancy's amateur portfolio, bulging with titles and records, was merely a warm-up act. She polished off the pros like she had no inkling of our best players' credentials. The fans and media were wide-eyed. She had game and she oozed charisma.

Nancy won a lot, but the big winner was the LPGA.

JoAnne Carner, who was on a victory run of her own—she won 23 tournaments in the 1970s—drew a laugh when she quipped, "We're all trying to steal Nancy's birth control pills, but so far we've been unsuccessful."

Little Known Facts

I've been called Miss Personality; been known as Miss Personality; described as Miss Personality. Oddly enough, folks rarely ask, "What do you think of the moniker, Marilynn?" Guess what? Given a choice I'd rather be known as a Goodwill Ambassador.

I traveled the globe as an ambassador, gave clinics, encouraged young women to consider golf careers, introduced men and women to the game of a lifetime. Doesn't that make me an ambassador?

Besides, if I'm an ambassador, I could be in line for an embassy.

•

To be fair, not everybody enjoyed my personality. One time a newspaper said, *Some temperamental girls claim that Marilynn's waves to the crowd and her exuberance after sinking a putt are distracting. But for every complaint, there are 100 ticket buyers who have come to watch 'Smitty' perform.*

I've always been gregarious. It's not an effort to smile. One of the most enjoyable things about the tour is meeting so many fine people.

•

Prior to the Muskogee Civitan Invitational in Oklahoma, the Sycamore Indian Tribe gave me the name Princess Personality Plus. Before the tournament each year, the Tribe honored one or two players. Betsy Rawls, Mickey Wright, Mary Lena Faulk and Beth Stone preceded me.

Now, that's a personality title I happily accept. And I treasure my headdress.

•

Five instructors deserve credit for my success, starting with Mike Murra, my first instructor and mentor, who introduced me to the game and nurtured me along. I will always be grateful for what he taught me. Without his instruction, I might never have had a career in professional golf and the ability to earn a living doing something I loved. But, even more, my life has been filled with joys and blessings that I attribute to his positive influence and friendship.

I learned a lot from Joe Norwood. The octogenarian pro at Los Angeles Country Club believed there should be no lower body movement. It seemed strange at first, but I hit the ball farther. He preached simplicity: the fewer parts to the swing, the fewer chances for error.

I participated in Joe's book, *Joe Norwood's Golf-O-Metrics With Marilynn Smith and Stanley Blicker: A Blueprint for a Perfect Swing from One of Golf's Most Famous Instructors.*

I worked with Harry Pressler, a California pro, quite a bit. He also taught Mickey Wright. He made sure that the forefinger and thumb of my right hand and the toe of the club pointed to the target on the follow-through. Thanks to Harry, I played some of my best golf. I always emphasize his theory when I teach.

When I lived in Florida, Gardner Dickinson lived nearby and I went to see him if my swing went haywire. He would come up with a solution in no time. Sometimes I tried to work things out myself, but I usually wound up tying myself in a knot. Gardner got me back on track—all it took was one key swing change.

I'd also like to credit Elmer Prieskorn, a soft-spoken man from Michigan who followed our Florida tour in the winter and worked with several LPGA players. I liked to talk golf with him. It was a great way to learn.

•

In 1965, I won the Betsy Rawls Peach Blossom Women's Open in Spartanburg, South Carolina and declared, "I'm no Champagne Tony Lema, but I'm ready to throw a beer party."

The next day a really wonderful newspaper item appeared:

Just before the presentation, Miss Smith said, "There's something about this town. I think it's the most wonderful town in America; the most wonderful golf course; the most wonderful people; the most wonderful everything." Isn't that just wonderful?

•

Computer-generated electronic scoreboards are common, but I remember how excited we were when Betty Hicks had a six-foot-by-three-foot wooden scoreboard roped to the top of her car—and how *Golf World* ran a story when we bought an aluminum scoreboard.

•

If a player wanted to grind down a wedge there was no such thing as an equipment trailer. The player just drove down the road and dragged the wedge on the pavement.

•

Somewhere along the line there was a movement to call us "proettes." Carol Mann, the LPGA president at the time, spoke out against the term. "It sounds like you're putting us down in comparison to the men," she said. "They're pros, we're proettes—it's so condescending. From now on, just call us pros, too. We don't care what some people think the term means. To us, it means professional, and that's what we are, professional golfers." Fortunately, "proettes" was short lived.

•

Today, pro-am parties are the norm. But they began during my presidency when the players suggested the idea.

•

In the 1960s, the men's tour prohibited its members from playing in an event with women. The rationale was: If you beat a girl, you're a bully. If she beats you, who is going to buy your clubs?

•

As a kid Mickey Wright used to sit on Gene Littler's golf bag and watch him hit practice balls at the La Jolla Country Club, outside San Diego. He was her childhood idol and hometown hero.

•

The LPGA is the longest running and oldest women's professional sports association.

•

Barbara Romack was the first female golfer to appear on a *Sports Illustrated* cover.

In 1961, she was the first female TV commentator at a woman's tournament, the LPGA Championship at the Stardust Country Club in Las Vegas.

She also did commentary at the 1968 U.S. Women's Open at Moselem Springs in Pennsylvania, teaming with Bud Palmer and Byron Nelson.

Barbara won the 1954 Women's Amateur and served as LPGA president in 1963.

World Traveler

In 1955, Fay Crocker, who was from Uruguay, and I conducted Spalding golf clinics and exhibitions in South America.

Fay approached a round of golf with flair, intenseness. She was an old-school stylist with a golf swing that drew praise from Bobby Jones.

Above all, she was a positive thinker who helped me immeasurably.

So here we were, boarding a 12-hour flight to Uruguay, Chile, Brazil and Columbia. I looked in the cockpit and saw the pilot, a big fellow—he could have been a Notre Dame fullback. First impressions are important; I knew we'd be safe.

After taking our seats I noticed two nuns across the aisle. Now, I'm not Catholic but it felt good to have them aboard—especially flying over the Amazon jungle. At one point, we were cruising about 30,000 feet in the air when one nun looked down and said, "See those lights? Smudge pots. There are cannibals down there." I looked out the window to make sure the plane's flaps weren't down.

I truly enjoyed South America. Fay spoke fluent Spanish so she took the lead when we conducted clinics and played exhibitions. I took Spanish in high school and knew enough words to communicate a bit. Check this: Hola, mi nombre es Marilynn, estoy encantado de conocerte.

Fay and I stayed with her parents in their lovely home in Montevideo, Uruguay. I appreciated their warm hospitality and her mom's home cooking was a treat. When we went to a soccer game the crowd recognized their local celebrity. They cheered and gave her a standing ovation. Ole!

•

We played a tournament in San Isidro near Guadalajara. I had it going in the last round—I was two-under and doing well—until I made eight at No.13. When you rattle shots around in the trees the locals call it 'playing the marimbas.'

•

In 1957, Wiffi Smith and I conducted golf demonstrations at U.S Air Force bases. One was at Aeroport de Paris-Orly, an air base south of Paris in France, another at Ramstein Air Force Base in Kaisersalutern, Germany. The trip was sponsored by the U.S. Air

Force to promote good will with American servicemen and their dependents.

Before Wiffi and I boarded a DC-3 they put a parachute on me— it didn't matter that I was wearing a dress. I rationalized, thinking, "Safety first, Marilynn. No time for modesty." Once they got me strapped in an airman said, "When you jump..." Not, "*If* you jump..." I was petrified. When we reached cruising altitude, Wiffi was comfortable, listening to music, about to fall asleep. I, on the other hand, was busy flying the plane. What a night.

Wiffi and I were grateful for the opportunity to conduct golf clinics for the USAF in Europe. They honored us with USAF Special Services plaques as tokens of appreciation.

Wiffi won the 1956 British Women's Amateur Open, the French Women's Amateur and the Trans-Mississippi Amateur before turning pro at the 1957 Jacksonville Open. She had eight LPGA wins to her credit when a wrist injury from a motorcycle accident ended her short, but brilliant career.

•

In the 1960s and 1970s Spalding was eager to assist the Ladies Golf Union of New Zealand and Australia promote ladies golf.

They sent me there many times to work with adult and junior lady golfers.

On one trip I met my namesake, Marilyn Smith. She was 12-years old at the time. Her dad was the golf pro at a club in Wellington, New Zealand. After she watched me conduct a clinic she told her dad, "I want to go to America and play on the LPGA tour like Marilynn Smith." Ten years later, there she was, playing as M.J. Smith (since I was still playing). She now teaches at the Army Navy Country Club in Arlington, Virginia. It is gratifying to know that Marilyn—a fine player and LPGA instructor—thinks I was instrumental in her career.

•

I went sightseeing in New Zealand and saw Mitre Peak, which, at 5,560 feet, is one of the world's highest mountains rising from the sea. I also saw Milford Sound, a spectacle created during the Ice Age when glaciers left sounds or fiords like Milford.

One thing about New Zealand that stays with me is this: There are sheep everywhere. They had something like 2.5 million people and 65 million sheep. (Recent numbers suggest there are over four million people and 40 million sheep.) I took pictures—roll after roll–of the countryside covered with sheep. Fotomat must have thought I was nuts.

•

In 1971, I went to Australia for the second time. I had been there two years earlier. I visited the farthest western city, Perth, population 611,000. They had the biggest flies I've ever seen—bigger than the ones in Texas—and fearless. I was giving a clinic and had trouble talking because they kept buzzing my mouth, trying to land on my lips.

I was in Warragul, a country town not far from Melbourne. After giving a demonstration, I played a nine-hole exhibition match with a young girl named Penny Pulz and Mrs. Lee Stanley, the Warragul women's golf champion. Penny was a 19-year old junior golfer. Burta Cheney, the head of the Victorian Ladies Golf Union, who started the first junior camp for girls, chose Penny Pulz to play with me. Today, Penny is a Class A member of the LPGA Tournament Division. She teaches in Phoenix, Arizona.

•

I was in Australia in 1974 for the first Australian Ladies Open. Staged by the Wills Tobacco Company. I compared the way it was run to the Masters, here at home, with good reason. Phil May, director of special promotions and Bob Wilson, Willis press relations director made several trips to the U.S. to observe our tournaments and tried to incorporate the best elements. The tournament was televised nationally and I was asked to commentate. Hopefully, I didn't mangle the jargon—they do have unique words and phrases. "G'Day" is hello; "ace" means excellent; "bull dust" is rubbish; something that "costs big bikkies" is expensive. Fortunately, a par is a par.

•

In addition to the countries I've mentioned, the game took me on an "Around the World" trip in 1969. I presented clinics and played golf exhibitions in the Philippines, Thailand, Malaysia and Japan.

I also gave golf lessons in Dallas, taught at the Bedford Springs Hotel in Pennsylvania and spent three months in the winter teaching at Runaway Bay Hotel & Golf Course in Jamaica. For three years in the early 1970s, I was the playing and teaching pro for the Yacht and Country Club at Stuart Florida.

•

I love to teach, the world has been my classroom. They say my lessons have reached more than 250,000 students. Along the way, I've probably hailed 8,597 cabs, tipped 11,415 bellhops and snagged at least half my clothing in suitcase zippers.

•

After retiring from the tour, I thought about unpacking and putting my feet up. But Dick Bigelow, a Philadelphia travel agent I met in the early 1950s at a Weathervane tournament, asked if I'd lead groups of amateur golfers on tours to places like Hawaii, Australia, New Zealand, Portugal and Casa de Campo in the Dominican Republic. Of course I would. Have clubs, will travel.

Making History in New Zealand

This story appeared in *Golf World*, March 4, 1969.

Marilynn Woos and Wows 'em in New Zealand:

World Tour Continues

By Bill Patterson

American professional golfer Marilynn Smith left New Zealand recently with two notable "firsts" to her credit as well as confirming her popularity in that country.

The U.S. LPGA star spent some six weeks in New Zealand from the start of the year and besides instructing became the first woman professional to play in a men's open tournament as well as the first woman to hit a golf ball across the Waikato River in the North Island city of Hamilton.

Miss Smith arrived in New Zealand from a layoff from the game this year to find herself thrust straight away into the Spalding Masters Open played on the picturesque Tauraga club course.

She was the only woman in the field of more than 80 professionals and amateurs which included the world's crack left-handed professional, Bob Charles, as well as two well performed NZ amateurs, Ross Murray and

Marilynn Smith

Stuart Jones, both of whom have finished well up in the individual placings in the Eisenhower international tournament. Murray was third in Rome.

The Spalding tournament was the start of the six day Bay of Plenty festival of golf which ended with the New Zealand PGA title event at Mount Maunganui—a beach resort only nine miles from Tauranga.

With the Spalding setting the tone for the week, which had attracted leading professionals from Australia and New Zealand in search of the PGA title, the first day was most important to the organizers.

It was therefore fortunate that Miss Smith could play and doubly fortunate that she was teamed with Jones and Charles in the first round.

This trio drew the biggest first day crowd—some 3,000—ever seen for the Bay of Plenty events and throughout the tournament the crowd kept faithful to the popular Miss Smith who had a 74 on the par 70 course—when playing off the men's tee.

Charles, who was to go on to win the tournament by 10 strokes as well as set a course record of 62, had a 66 and Jones a 69.

Miss Smith finished the four-round event with a total of 297 comprising rounds of 74, 76, 73 and 74, and found herself struggling a bit to find form again, especially as most of her second shots were taken from well behind her opponents.

As far as New Zealand officials could ascertain it was not only definitely the first time that a professional woman player had taken part in such a tournament but also the first time for a U.S. woman professional since the 1940s when Babe Zaharias, the triple Olympic medalist had taken part in a similar tournament.

Miss Smith, who confessed afterward that she felt that men's professional golf was not the place for women as it was "not fair to the men," also played the first shot in the New Zealand PGA tournament before leaving Tauranga for her teaching tour of New Zealand.

She conducted instruction clinics for promising young players at Christchurch, Palmerston North, and Hamilton as well as playing in six exhibition matches in which she partnered leading New Zealand players and won five.

It was while in Hamilton that she was induced, along with NZPGA captain Frank Buckler, to attack the Waikato River drive, a distance of more than 230 yards from the point in the middle of the city where the shots were taken.

Her effort was not made any easier that she had only a narrow sight passage through the trees on the bank, but after clipping off a branch she *fired her next right across the river where once Maori warriors exchanged shots with European settlers.*

Miss Smith's shots were not so deadly but they did give rise to some concern among rowers practicing on the river for a regatta.

Throughout her tour of New Zealand Miss Smith enhanced the popularity she had attained on her previous visit and again proved one of the finest ambassadors of overseas golf that this country has seen.

No trouble was too great for her. Her popularity was shown in the exhibition she gave at the tiny South Island town of Alexandria (pop. 2,920); she had a gallery of more than 2,000 following her play.

Golf is the fastest growing sport in New Zealand and women's golf especially has a strong following and the New Zealand Ladies Golf Union action in bringing Miss Smith here has been widely praised with regard to the clinics that she conducted for the young players.

One of these players Heather Booth, who is the reigning British Match play titleholder and has played with success in Florida, more than impressed Miss Smith who would like this champion and some of the other leading NZ youngsters to try the Florida amateur circuit in what is New Zealand's off season.

The NZ women's team record in the Espirito Santo event has not been good and far from matching the men in international amateur competition and this is due mainly to the lack of hard tournament play at home and overseas.

A visit to the United States for some of the major amateur events could be just the answer to remedying this situation.

Miss Smith also found the hardest hitter in women's golf that she has encountered, in New Zealand, when she met the national stroke play titleholder, Una Wickham who has been known to hit around the 300-yard mark off the tee.

While in Hamilton Miss Smith also made a fan in the Bay of Plenty Orange Festival Queen, Sue Cornwell, of Rotorua.

In a chance encounter with the Orange Queen, Miss Smith discovered that she was due to visit the United States in March for the National Orange Show at San Bernardino and she gave the young Bay beauty welcome introductions to friends in Los Angeles where Sue will be spending some time.

Before leaving New Zealand for Australia, the Far East, and Europe, Miss Smith said she would like to come back for a holiday and New Zealand golf enthusiasts are hoping there will not be another five year break before she returns.

Still on the Go

My world tour began December 26, 1968. It covered New Zealand, Australia, Singapore, Bangkok, Manila and Japan.

It was tiring and, I suppose most people would have been happy to head home and relax for a few weeks. Not me. I looked forward to a two-month holiday in Hong Kong, New Delhi, Agra, Tel Aviv, Jerusalem, Haifa, Athens, Rome, Florence, West Berlin and London.

I enjoy cultural differences, always eager to experience more. Israel was fabulous. The people were vibrant and interested in meeting Americans.

The food was a culinary pleasure in several countries. I don't recall exactly what they served in India, but I liked it. I remember everybody was thin … slender. One thing that struck me funny was seeing cows walking in the street. Right down the middle of the road—without a license plate.

When I was in India during the cold war my American patriotism got the better of me. Two Russian generals walked straight toward me one day … and I didn't budge. They had to walk around me. That was in Agra when I visited the Taj Mahal, a stunning white domed mausoleum regarded as one of the eight wonders of the world. It actually glistens and depending on the time of day, changes colors.

I've sure done my share of traveling. I may hold the record for the most times a woman set her watch to correspond with local time. Then again, I'm not sure what 'local' means. I wasn't in any one place long enough to consider it local.

I visited Japan twice for golf clinics and exhibitions. The first time, the National Golf Foundation sent me to Japan with Gary Wiren, one of my all-time favorite gentlemen. He is a golf educator, a PGA Master Professional and a former national PGA staff director. He told me that he was in a South Florida long-driving contest and he came in first, belting one 381 yards and one foot. That would wow them in Japan.

We were there for two weeks. Gary's unique blend of entertainment and historical knowledge gave the presentations a new dimension. I remember a clinic in Tokyo. There were 1,000 people inside a big auditorium. We had an interpreter so it lasted quite a while because we had to wait while what we said was relayed in Japanese, but everybody enjoyed it. Gary's teaching was effective, but I have no idea how the interpreter kept up with my patter.

Sometime after that, a Japanese company invited me back for more clinics. I was impressed with Japanese women golfers. They weren't long hitters but their form was good and they were eager to learn the finer points of the game. I said at the time that I wouldn't be surprised to see Japanese professionals on the U.S. Tour.

Sure enough, Ayako Okamoto joined the LPGA tour in 1981. She had a remarkable career. She won 62 tournaments internationally, including 17 LPGA events, and was inducted into the World Golf Hall of Fame.

I visited a U.S. Army hospital in Tokyo to cheer U.S. servicemen wounded in Vietnam. It's an honor, a true privilege to spend time with them. Having been ill and confined to my hotel room for a few days, the soldiers actually cheered me up as much I did them. We talked about golf and they had a slew of questions that led to mini bedside clinics. It all went well—until they asked about my putting. Touchy subject. I'd rather chip balls into a bedpan than demonstrate my putting stroke.

A soldier asked if I let a bogey get me down. Here I was talking to a wounded man who wouldn't let a war injury get him down. It puts things in perspective.

The president of a Japanese broadcasting company took me to a geisha house for dinner one evening and invited me to his house for dinner another evening. I took my shoes off and sat on the floor. His wife was a marvelous lady. The food she made was fresh and delicious. I maneuvered my chopsticks like I was giving myself a golf lesson: Keep your thumb and index finger pointing to the target, Marilynn, and follow through. I was about a 10-handicap with rice. But I'd trade sake for a beer, any day.

I rode the Bullet Train from Tokyo to Osaka. It was the second generation—introduced for the 1964 Olympic games—radically different and more than twice as fast as the original train. This one had a top speed of 210 mph; the average speed was 101 mph, about the speed of a pro's golf awing. We sped past telephone poles like a driver going through a tee shot.

Golf in Japan was far different than anything I had ever experienced. The caddies were women—caddy-sans, they called them—who wore white hats that looked like pillowcases. Some seemed quite mature, well into a career. There was one caddy-san per foursome and she took care of everything. She fetched clubs— even selected the proper one after gauging our ability. She tested wind currents, read greens, cleaned our golf balls and replaced them with the lettering pointed toward the direction the putt would break.

I watched maintenance workers trimming the fringe around greens by hand, with garden shears … clippers. And they seemed to use the same clippers to prune trees.

Between nines the Japanese took a one-hour lunch break. Then they played the back nine and retired to a Japanese bath.

Golf was slow, dignified, and just about an all day affair. They *really* like the game.

Oh, I'll never forget the triple-decker driving ranges. They are something else, and crowded—you have to have a starting time to hit balls.

I'm not much for heights, but it must be exciting to be on the second level and see golf balls whizzing above and below you. It would be fun if everybody teed up a ball and an announcer gave a countdown: Three … two … one … WHAM: Let it rain golf balls.

I gave a clinic at Tokyo's Shiba Park Driving Range. From my vantage point I felt like I was on stage at the Kennedy Center.

Mickey Wright

I competed with several extraordinary players whose accomplishments have withstood the test of time. One player, Mickey Wright, exemplified women's golf. Ben Hogan and Byron Nelson, no less, admired her swing saying it was the best they had ever seen.

Great golf swings—be they a man's or a woman's—are still compared with Mickey's. But they are runners-up, at best. She was that good.

She wasn't interested in stop-and-chats with the gallery, she showed up for work. I benefitted when I was paired with her because the rhythm of her swing made me a better player. I watched and emulated. It was like wearing earphones, listening to the New York Philharmonic play Strauss and responding to the tempo.

Betsy Rawls marveled at her ability. "I always say Mickey was the best golfer the LPGA ever had," she said. "I think most of the people who saw her play still think that."

Kathy Whitworth agreed. "I relished those days when I was paired with Mickey. It was so much fun and so exciting to watch her play. She was great."

That's quite a statement coming from a golfer who won more tournaments than any professional golfer, man or woman. From 1961 to 1985, Kathy won 88 official events and was named LPGA Player of the Year seven times.

Mickey joined the tour in 1955 and won 82 times even though she cut her schedule back significantly after 1969. She was only a part-time player for more than five years.

In 1960, Mickey won the first tournament of the year, the Sea Island Invitational, and went on to dominate the decade with 68 victories—13 of them in 1963, a record that still stands.

I've done the math many times and still shake my head. It seems impossible, particularly since Mickey was bothered with wrist tendonitis as early as 1965.

She won 13 majors: four U.S. Women's Opens, four LPGA Championships, two Titleholders and three Women's Western Opens. She won the Vare Trophy five times and was the LPGA leading money winner four times. She is the only woman to hold all four major titles at the same time.

How good was she? Well, Kathy Whitworth said Mickey could have won 100 tournaments if she hadn't quit early.

Many of our tour stops were in small towns and word of her victory splurge preceded her. Local writers picked up on it and made her the runaway favorite—all but assuring victory before she laced her golf shoes. That pressure was more than she bargained for.

Mickey was never comfortable when it came to media matters or public appearances. She is and was a very private person. I believe she is entitled to that.

Mickey came along at a crucial time. Babe wasn't booming drives anymore, the marquee needed a name that could draw klieg lights and adoring fans.

As good as that sounds, Lennie Wirtz, the LPGA tournament director was in a bind. Yes, Mickey provided new star power, but she started winning *everything* and Lennie had trouble finding enough players to fill out the field. If he could lower the winner's share from 20 percent to 15 percent, he reasoned there would be more money to go around. Mickey agreed because she knew it would help the tour.

My career hit its stride in 1963 when I edged Mickey Wright in a playoff to win the Titleholders at Augusta Country Club. The Titleholders was to the LPGA what the Masters is to the men's tour and Mickey was the number one player in the world. She was genuinely gracious as she hugged and congratulated me.

I was a major champion, at last. I hummed a medley of Strauss waltzes the rest of the year and won three more times.

As I write this, the United States Golf Association Museum just unveiled the Mickey Wright Room where more than 200 personal artifacts are displayed. It is only the fourth such gallery—the first dedicated to a woman. The others honor Bob Jones, Ben Hogan and Arnold Palmer.

Rare air and exquisite company, for sure. The United States Golf Association has rightfully awarded her the Key to the Game.

Left: I represented Ping late in my career and even after I retired. The Solheim family are wonderful friends.

Below: This photo shows one of my key golf tips. Harry Pressler, who also taught Mickey Wright, made sure the forefinger and thumb of my right hand and the toe of the club pointed to the target on the follow through. Excellent advice that I stressed in my clinics when I taught golf around the world.

Karsten Solheim, president of Ping, and Ben Hogan with an admirer clutching her hero's arm at the Marilynn Smith Founders' Classic—the first Womens' Senior Tournament.

Dolores Hope, an honorary member of the LPGA and generous contributor to the LPGA Foundation, with me.

Photo courtesy of David Ashworth

World Golf Hall of Fame trophy. It has each member's signature etched in the glass. My prized possession.

Left: Each member of the World Golf Hall of Fame has a locker. I represented Ping late in my career and into retirement. The green argyle socks go with the plus-fours I wore when I led golf tours.

Below: Many artifacts, even my bible, are on display in my World Golf Hall of Fame exhibit. The golf bag represents 27 consecutive one-year contracts with Spalding.

Upper left: With Kathy Whitworth who presented me at the World Golf Hall of Fame in 2006.

Upper right: LPGA members and teaching pros Mary Lou Crocker and Renee Powell at the ceremony.

Lower left: Behind the 18th green at the 2011 RR Donnelley Founders Cup tournament. Standing: Shirley Spork and Karrie Webb. Seated Louise Suggs and me.

Below right: Standing: MJ Smith (my name sake from New Zealand and Louise Suggs. Seated with me is Carolyn Bivens, former LPGA Commissioner.

I was blessed to have so many friends, relatives and LPGA professionals in attendance at my World Golf Hall of Fame induction ceremony.

Above: A tee shot with persimmon, and a putt with body English.
Below: Golf in Spain, where I led a golf tour.

(l-r) With my niece Michele Alexander, brother-in-law Clifford Pappas, sister Gay Pappas and niece Marilynn Leahy.

World Golf Hall of Fame Class of 2006.(l-r) Larry Nelson, Henry Picard, Marilynn Smith, Mark McCormack and Vijay Singh.

My Finest Hour

I won the Titleholders twice, in a row, edging Mickey Wright both times—which was like going five-for-five against Koufax, catching the winning pass in a Super Bowl, starring in a blockbuster movie with Clark Gable and getting top billing.

When I beat Mickey by a shot in a playoff at the 1963 Titleholders, we were tied with 292 totals after 72 holes of regulation play. I trailed in the playoff by three shots after thirteen holes, but mounted a comeback to draw even. Then I hit a career second shot at eighteen—a three-iron that finished eight feet from the hole. My putt won the championship by one stroke, 72-73.

I told reporters that I never hit the ball better—and meant it.

Mickey says that day was her most memorable moment with me. At the time, she was not only the defending champion, she was bidding for her third consecutive Titleholders crown. If she feels that way, it truly defines her character. I was happy to win, but hated to beat Mickey, and told her so.

The Titleholders was our second playoff of the year—Mickey beat me at the St. Petersburg Open.

I repeated as Titleholders champion the next year, 1964, thanks to a second-round course record 35-31—66, again edging Mickey by a shot. As it turned out, the 66 was my career best.

Wearing the green jacket was a privilege. It meant more to me than the $1,300 first prize check.

I started the final day with a three-stroke lead—far from comfortable with Mickey Wright in second place.

She got back to even at the tenth hole, thanks to an approach shot that finished six inches from the hole and a birdie putt. I was in the group ahead. We stayed even until I reached the par-three fourteenth. My tee shot landed six feet past the pin.

Just before I stepped up to putt, a roar went up from the gallery at thirteen—Mickey made another birdie. I made my birdie putt and that was the turning point. If I missed, I would have been one-down with four holes to play.

I took a one-stroke lead when Mickey's tee shot at fourteen ended up in a bunker and she made bogey. We parred out from there.

It had to be the greatest golfing week of my life. But it wasn't easy.

My 289 total was two strokes better than Patty Berg's tournament record 291. And I equaled the 54-hole record of 216 that I set in 1963. My second round 66 was two shots better than Patty Berg's record 68 in 1955. And my second nine 31, broke Kathy Cornelius' record 33 in 1961. I made my first birdie at the par-five eighth hole. Then I one-putted seven of the next nine holes, six of them for birdies.

MARILYNN'S ROUND

Par Out	444	353	454—36
Smith Out	444	353	444—35
Par In	453	435	444—36—72
Smith In	342	434	344—31—66

TITLEHOLDERS
In The Money

Marilynn Smith	73-66-77-73—289	$1,300.00
Mickey Wright	74-70-75-71—290	1,000.00
Betsy Rawls	71-77-74-72—294	800.00
Ruth Jessen	77-72-74-73—296	625.00
Judy Kimball	71-72-78-75—296	625.00
Clifford Ann Creed	75-69-79-74—297	500.00
Shirley Englehorn	75-75-73-74—297	500.00
Mary Mills	74-74-78-72—298	400.00
Louise Suggs	73-73-76-77—299	350.00
Marlene Hagge	75-72-78-75—300	250.00
Sandra Haynie	74-75-76-75—300	250.00
Judy Torluemke	75-73-76-76—300	250.00
JoAnn Prentice	72-72-77-80—301	175.00
Gloria Armstrong	72-75-78-78—303	150.00
Patty Berg	69-76-79-80—304	81.25
Andy Cohn	74-76-80-74—304	81.25
Carol Mann	75-74-80-75—304	81.25
Barbara Romack	74-72-78-80—304	81.25

Out Of The Money

Peggy Wilson	76-71-78-80—305
Wiffi Smith	78-76-76-75—305
Patsy Hahn	74-77-80-76—307
Kathy Cornelius	76-74-80-78—308
Murle Lindstrom	77-76-76-79—308
Beth Stone	78-73-80-78—309
Betty Jameson	80-77-77-75—309
Sandra McClinton	77-77-80-75—309
Kathy Whitworth	81-78-78-73—310
Sybil Griffin	79-76-81-76—312
Gloria Fecht	74-76-82-80—312
Peggy Kirk Bell	77-79-78-80—314
Sherry Wheeler	77-75-84-79—315
*Polly Riley	82-74-83-76—315
Shirley Spork	75-81-84-78—318
*Barbara White	79-79-83-77—318
Sandra Spuzich	79-81-82-80—322
*Mrs. Harton Semple	82-75-85-81—323
*Marge Burns	81-82-81-79—323
*Mrs. Richard Garlington	84-81-82-83—330
Amy Amizich	82-86-86-79—333
*Grace Lyons Clay	85-83-84-85—337
Mary Lena Faulk	79-73-79-WD
*Eileen Stulb	80-82-WD
*Mrs. Jerry Covich	99-95-WD

* Amateur.

The Defining Moment

The year was 1972. The man was David Foster, president of the Colgate Company, who put the LPGA on page one of every section except the classifieds when he launched the Colgate Dinah Shore Winner's Circle Championship. We made local news, national news, sports news, and entertainment news. We were a main attraction.

It was the richest tournament in LPGA history. The prize money totaled $110,000. *Sports Illustrated* called him a fiscal angel.

Colgate's products were primarily directed toward women and David Foster recognized that women's golf was a perfect way to communicate with Colgate's key market segment. "Our company has made a commitment to women's sports," he said, "because women's participation has been neglected too long. Our ultimate goal is to see women gain equal stature and recognition when sports projects are planned—at all levels of competition, professional and amateur."

After crisscrossing the country for years, we reached our Street of Dreams: Madison Avenue. At last, big business, a Fortune 500 Company, invested their marketing and advertising dollars in an

LPGA tournament. Women's golf was on corporate radar screens. Things were falling in place.

Sports Illustrated called it *a golf tournament that is to the women what the talkies were to the movies.*

Our focus was about to shift dramatically from small town venues to larger metropolitan areas.

The Colgate-Dinah Shore was a treat for the players. We were ecstatic about the potential payout. And we had Dinah Shore. Not only did she love to play golf, she cherished her namesake tournament.

The celebrity pro-am was dazzling. It was easy to get swept up in the excitement. The interaction between sports and celebrity was big box office. Stars, big names, like Bob Hope, Frank Sinatra, Jack Lemmon, Clint Eastwood, Jackie Gleason, Rita Hayworth, Perry Como and James Garner brought their clubs. The pro-am, alone, stimulated interest in women's golf. Dinah's presence appealed to network executives and that triggered more TV coverage. Other corporations paid attention. They saw the potential benefits of aligning with the LPGA to showcase their products and services.

•

Somewhere there is a newspaper photo from the Dinah Shore tournament. It shows me getting chipping pointers from the golf pro at Mission Hills Country Club in Rancho Mirage, California. You may have heard of him—Ken Venturi.

Dinah

The Colgate-Dinah Shore Winner's Circle was dubbed a major in 1983 and has since undergone six name changes—including the 2000 version when they did the unmentionable. They dropped Dinah's name and called it the Nabisco Championship.

Well, that may do for some, but the rest of us continue to call it the Dinah Shore, as we have from day one.

Dinah was America's darling twenty years before she opened corporate boardrooms for the LPGA. Chevrolet sponsored her television show and the Chevy jingle was America's theme song. "See the USA in your Chevrolet, America is asking you to call. Drive your Chevrolet through the USA, America's the greatest land of all." Dinah sang it, we sang along and she finished by blowing a big smooch to the audience. (I'm singing it right now.)

Sorry, a tear just welled up because Dinah's name is missing from the tournament. I mean, would they drop U.S. from the U.S. Open?

Dinah was an avid golfer. Her popularity as a singer and television personality, combined with her love of the game made her the perfect tournament host—and she was vibrant in the role.

Dinah took the tournament seriously. It was her way of making a statement. She said, "Women want to be attractive, they want to be able to participate. If you want to look good on the golf course, you've got to stay in shape. If you want to hit the ball you've got to practice. I think our tournament has given women a good image of themselves, which I think is important."

She brought more to the table than just her tournament, much more. She brought fashion to the table. She set new standards for women's golf and women golfers. The trend was visible, coast-to-coast via television. And you could note improvement from year to year.

It was no longer acceptable to wear just anything on a golf course. Personal grooming, diet, sunblock protection and attractive makeup were part of the equation. The players discussed new creams, new grooming products with her—we became more conscious.

Her popularity attracted women to the game. Young girls responded to the glamour factor; they dedicated themselves to careers as touring professionals.

I asked about Dinah's biggest tournament moment. "One year," she said, "I was eight-under par for my pro-am team on my ball."

What were her scores like? "An 85 is really good. If I break 90, I send up a flare."

Dinah wasn't always at her best during the pro-am because she talked to the fans, signed autographs and posed for pictures between shots. "I am always the last one to get to the tee," she confessed. It hardly mattered.

The tournament changed her life. She said, "No matter where I am or what I'm doing I make sure my schedule has an extra day for golf."

She invited LPGA players to appear on her television show, even got us roles in commercials. She was the first female member of Hillcrest Country Club in Los Angeles. Dinah is a member of the World Golf Hall of Fame and an honorary member of the LPGA Hall of Fame. She received the Old Tom Morris Award from the Golf Course Superintendents Association of America, their highest award.

Dinah's life-size statue stands near the eighteenth hole at Mission Hills Country Club—a gift from George Montgomery, her ex-husband.

Kathy Whitworth and I filmed an Ajax commercial (one of Colgate's first cleaning products). I remember the Ajax jingle: "Use

Ajax, the foaming cleanser, cleans your sink just like a whiz. Use Ajax, the foaming cleanser, floats the dirt right down the drain."

The script called for us to demonstrate the product by removing a stain—with some sort of government watchdog present to make sure it was legit. Talk about pressure. It took four hours to get it right.

Marilynn and Kathy in kitchen

Marilynn to camera as Kathy cleans	Marilynn: I don't care if it's a golf game or a cleaning product. To be a champion you need that competitive edge.
Holds up product	That's why I use Ajax.
Puts Ajax on stain	Ajax helps wipe out the toughest food stains, faster than Comet.
Starts demo.	
Stain is gone. Water goes down the drain	Kathy: And it even has grease cutters that help stop grease from building up in drains.
Marilynn, to camera	Now, if only I had that Ajax edge every time I played golf.

Kathy, joking with Marilynn	You'd beat me every time.
Kathy and Marilynn laugh	
Product shot	Announcer: Watch Kathy and Marilynn in the Colgate-Dinah Shore Golf Championship. Ajax for stains and drains.

Ladies and Gentlemen

In 1974, I was the guest speaker at the Women's Metropolitan Golf Association's annual meeting in New York. This is from their newsletter:

Marilynn Smith, our guest speaker—compliments of Colgate-Palmolive Company—one of the top women professionals in LPGA history, and a commentator for ABC during this year's U.S. Open at Oakmont, was presented by Mrs. Wilson.

Marilynn suddenly had a lot of competition from a grandfather's clock chiming, and a temperamental microphone. However, she took this in stride and announced, "Hairdos are important to golf. I had mine cut yesterday." (Applause) "Do you really like it?" (More applause) "When I looked into the mirror this morning I wasn't sure it was me." She then started speaking but stopped abruptly and said, "How do I know what you want to hear? How about you telling me?"

The response was great and naturally there were many questions about becoming a professional, the trials and tribulations of traveling and playing. What else? The golf swing, mental attitude, and does one lose desire after many years of competition. All questions were answered with sincerity and appropriate quips. The membership participation was outstanding. When Marilynn took an iron and moved in front of the dais to show some basics of the swing many left their seats and crowded in close for instructions. Time was short or many of us would have stayed for hours.

Bumps in the Road, and the Air

World travel can be confusing. Take a trip from Los Angeles to Auckland, New Zealand, for instance. That's a long haul. When you get off the plane your body isn't sure if it's yesterday, today or tomorrow. Your stomach doesn't know whether to brace itself for a poached egg, or meatloaf.

One time my plane hit so many air pockets that I felt like I was driving a car down a flight of steps. I was woozy when I got to the hotel. Those were my white-knuckle days. They had to pour two glasses of champagne in me before I'd board the plane. The flight attendant's announcement that my seat cushion will act as a floatation device didn't help, either.

I flew from Los Angeles to Australia and New Zealand so many times that you'd think I didn't mind all the hours in the air. Phooey, I was scared to death.

Auckland is 19 hours *ahead* of L.A. I got there on Friday at two in the afternoon, but I felt like I was still in L.A, where it was seven o'clock Thursday evening. If that doesn't give you the yips, nothing will.

It took me three days to get over jet lag. I'd get to my destination and want to go to bed. But I was told, no, stay awake and get with the time. That was tough, really tough.

I never found a way to regulate my diet to ease the time difference. Instead, I was a vitamin nut. Marlene Hagge and I used to take copious amounts of vitamins—I took twenty different pills. I kept a big bagful of vitamins with me to help fight off infection.

Sometimes I coped with rugged schedules. In Hawaii during a 1951 visit I gave 16 exhibitions in 12 days.

People wonder how I could possibly exist living out of a suitcase so much. I guess it was my enthusiasm for life, meeting people, communicating and learning about their lives. I've always been a people person—that, and my curiosity kept me going.

In a calendar year there was little down time when I was actually home. Just the holidays in December, and then I was off again.

Here's a good one: In all my travels on the LPGA circuit and doing clinics and exhibitions around the world, I can't recall ever having a kitchen where I could cook a meal. The fact is I'm not a cook. My mother was a terrific cook so I was always glad to get home and enjoy her food.

One more oddity: I washed my clothes in motel bathtubs. I never went to Laundromats. My motel room had wet clothes draped over the furniture, lampshades, curtain rods and bedposts. There's nothing like a room with 100 percent humidity.

Allow me to paint a word picture: It was a beautiful day in Guadalajara as I relaxed on the balcony of my hotel room writing thank you notes. Here's another one: My balcony overlooked scenic Melbourne. The gentle breeze felt refreshing as I penned thank you notes to the folks who hosted our event. Would you believe that, in each case, while I was scribbling away I was soaking laundry in the washbasin?

Tour life had a glamorous side. We attended parties, played golf with wonderful people, were celebrated at tour stops. We appeared on talk shows, endorsed golf equipment and signed autographs. You should have seen us with our hair in curlers doing laundry, or crammed in cars with all our possessions and 40,000 delightful miles of mostly two-lane roads in our future. You know what? I wouldn't trade it for any other career. The same can be said for the others who shared the journey.

Lessons Learned

My greatest lesson learned is: Keep your emotions under control. If you get frustrated after a shot and throw a club or swear, your enemies will be happy to see you make a fool of yourself and your friends will feel sorry for you. Etiquette is so important. We all get frustrated because we want to do better. But try not to let your frustration show. Keep it close to your chest.

•

Mike Murra, my first golf coach, would have been proud that his student had 'made it' when I was inducted into the World Golf Hall of Fame. He was a great encourager and cheered me on to many tournament victories. We spent hours and hours on the driving range going over swing fundamentals. He was extremely patient.

Mike's lessons went well beyond the finer points of the golf swing. He helped me learn to be myself. He warned against getting a 'big head'. Sportsmanship, courtesy and respect were as important to Mike as a long drive, or a birdie putt.

•

My dad wrote to me in 1956. "It was good to talk to you last night, but I felt sorry about your round of golf. I am sure you will find it a big help if you eat some sugar between rounds. It will give you that quick pickup which is so essential. I know lots of golfers who carry a lump of sugar with them and eat it occasionally to keep up their energy. Matt Palacio was one who did it. So your old man says keep sugar with you at all times and use it."

My energy level picked up, but it didn't help my putting.

•

Writing thank-you notes was routine and a pleasure, after each event. It was never a chore. My mother taught me that a note is always welcomed. Her guidance has served me well through the years.

When I traveled for Spalding, I wrote thank-you notes to the people who worked at our last event whether it was a tournament or a golf clinic—from committee members to ladies locker room attendants. I took the time to tell each one how their efforts made the event a success.

When Shirley Spork and I traveled together the one in the passenger seat wrote thank you notes. I still write letters and send cards and thank-you notes. I've been told that I keep the post office in business. It has also been said that I buy ink by the gallon and postage stamps by the pound.

•

I was pleased to learn that LPGA Commissioner Mike Whan's staff informs the players before each tournament about the event's sponsors, their purpose in participating and the benefits they expect to achieve. The players receive names and addresses so they can write thank-you notes.

Excellent public relations move.

Bits and Pieces

This and that from clippings, jottings and memory:

Golf World July 21, 1948

At Lawrence Kansas, coeds, and some of the male students were aware that Marilynn (correct spelling) Smith, although just a freshman at the University of Kansas, is quite a gal. When Marilynn went to the final round of the Woman's National Collegiate golf championship at the Ohio State University course in Columbus, she made her first impression in national golf.

Miss Smith lost to Miss Grace Lenczyk of Florida's John B. Stetson University, two-up, but competent critics rate her as one of the promising young women golfers. She arrived for the collegiate championship as a little known entry, but her qualifying score of 74, third in the field, created attention. So did her sparkling personality. GOLF WORLD correspondent Roger E. Gaylord of Dartmouth College, a Columbus newspaperman during his summer holidays, said, "She has the best swing I have seen and is good all the way. As far as I can see all she needs is a little more experience. She was visibly shaky for her first few holes against Miss Lenczyk. I also found out that she is a terrific dancer."

I could add more, but why dilute the punch line?

•

Louise Suggs was sorting through her mail and found a letter from a fan who wanted her to settle a bet he made with a friend. "My friend says you, Babe and Patty decide in advance who's going to win tournaments. I bet he's wrong." Betsy Rawls asked, "What are you going to tell him?" Louise said, "I'm going to ask if he's ever seen three cats fight over a plate of fish."

•

Margie Masters was the first Australian to join the LPGA tour. She said she had trouble adjusting to American beer, American men and American caddies.

She thought the beer and men were terrific, but the caddies, especially ones with a southern drawl, were a problem. "I can't understand a word they say," she complained. "And I never know what's going to happen next. One caddie showed up with a bandaged hand. He said he was cut up in a knife fight. Another called from the city jail and asked if I would pay his $700 bond." That ended his career. She wasn't interested in a caddie on loan from the Sheriff's Department.

•

Carol Mann before teeing off in a tournament: "I've got to win $350 here. I've got car payments, dentist bills—all that stuff. I could concentrate on my golf better if I wasn't concentrating on not throwing up."

•

Cathy Duggan four-putted during the Houston tourney and was lamenting to partner Kathy Ahern that, "I hit a good putt." Kathy asked, "Which one?"

•

A viewer criticized Judy Rankin. "On the Dinah Shore telecast you're playing professional golf one minute and the next minute you've got your elbows in soap suds in a Colgate commercial. Isn't that inconsistent?"

Judy replied, "Well, let me tell you, that is the real me. I'm a female athlete—and a wife and mother. I do dishes, I wash clothes, and I drive kids to school. There's no reason women athletes can't be women, too. I think I'm more liberated than all the liberated women in the world. I'm doing what most of the women in the world would like to do. I have a home and a family, and still have an opportunity to earn a good living at what I like to do."

•

Patty Berg and I were near the end of a round in St. Louis on a hot, humid day. It was downright muggy. You could grab a handful of air and wring it out. My face was soaked with perspiration as I surveyed a 35-foot putt. The caddie removed the flagstick, walked about four feet from the cup and stood, holding the pin with one hand. I lined up my putt—aiming at the flagstick, not the hole. It was just an instant, but you know how those things go. Once you realize how goofy you look, surrounded by a gallery, it seems a lot longer. I made the putt, thank you for asking.

•

A reporter told the world about our secrets:

Everyone must have a weekly beauty shop appointment, and for those with problem hair, it's twice a week. Nylon shirts have been banned on the course for the top-heavy (too revealing), and a few bottom-heavies have received polite suggestions about culottes and golf skirts.

•

Clothing styles were the topic of conversation at the 1970 U.S. Women's Open. "Girlish garb," as Linda Craft called it, had come into vogue. It was actually a mini-skirt movement and the consensus considered it a step in the right direction. Linda, a member of the LPGA publicity committee, said, "It goes back to the rugged days of Babe Zaharias." She noted, "Short skirts are in fashion. The only problem is when I bend over to study a putt the gallery gets an eyeful." That was corrected with culottes. Most agreed they were comfortable and feminine.

"We're women first and pro golfers second," said Donna Caponi. "A lot of girls look darling in their short skirts. I wore a white dress Sunday, and when I walked into the clubhouse a fellow asked, 'Where are you going all dressed up?' 'Dressed up?' I replied. 'I just came off the course.' It made me feel great because I didn't look like an athlete."

Carol Mann would wear a blue print jersey golf dress with a touch of blue eye shadow and a matching bow in her hair.

I wore calf-length skirts for many years. Then, in the 1960s, my hemline began to creep up—to be fashionable—until it was above my knees. Some economists talk about the "Hemline Theory" which suggests that women's hemlines rise along with stock prices. Once the players started wearing hot pants, all bets were off.

•

Newspaper clipping:

Probably the worst crisis Marilynn has faced this year was at the Pleasant Valley Country Club in Sutton, MA, a regular stop on the LPGA tour. As she stepped onto the putting green, JoAnne Carner was already there—wearing the same skirt. Among the Lipstick Set, that's worse than a double bogey.

•

Carol Mann to a reporter about dating and marriage: "You know, you've got to quit this life while you're still young, and not spend too much time thinking about getting married. This isn't a natural way of life, but you can build up security in it and get stuck here. So I'm looking—and I really mean that. Right now, I'm on re-runs."

•

From a *Golf World* letter to the editor:

I only subscribe to your magazine because you do acknowledge the LPGA. But must you have that AWFUL Marilynn Smith on your staff? All she can write about are the old battle-axes and her self.

Well, at least she spelled my name right.

•

I have to laugh at this clip:

Judy Torluemke, the All-American girl, lovely with brown hair, freckles and no makeup, a child golf prodigy who grew into one of the top women golfers was playing her second to last tournament before retiring to become Mrs. Y. P. Rankin. At 22, she was a five-year-veteran of the tour.

Well, not exactly. She went on to win 26 LPGA titles, topped the money list in 1976 and 1977. Judy Rankin is a member of the World Golf Hall of Fame, was LPGA Player of the Year twice and received the Bob Jones Award, the highest honor given by the USGA in recognition of distinguished sportsmanship in golf. An ailing back ended her competitive days but launched a TV career as a highly respected on-course commentator.

Footnote: Judy really did plan to retire after losing in the second round of the British Women's Amateur. But within a few weeks *Sports Illustrated* called to say they planned to put her on the cover of the U.S. Women's Open issue. That got her back on tour.

Bravo—to the person who made the call.

•

Donna Caponi, explaining why she plumb-bobs with her putter on the green: "I'm checking to see if the putter shaft is straight.

•

Dick Taylor, who wrote for *Golf World* told it like it was. This is from a piece he wrote in 1970.

They zing four-wood shots into par-4 greens with the aplomb of a male star hitting a nine-iron. The distaff side doesn't get those long shots as close to the hole most of the time, and because viva la difference they don't have the same putting concentration. But they are stellar performers somewhat shrouded in anonymity that comes from playing in non-metropolitan areas often, and lack of television.

They also are a somewhat prideful and stubborn lot, setting up the courses they play themselves, from the men's tees, with pin placements Joe Dey would grade A, resulting in few sub-70 rounds which the nation's news media has been feeding upon for years via the men's circuit. Sandra Haynie charging to a par-72 score and victory won't thrill a busy make-up man in a sports department on Sunday night when baseball scores are flowing and the men's pro golf report is being rapidly filed, chock full of 65s and the lot.

But the gals continue to delight a small, but loyal section of golf buffs who annually look forward to their arrival. And why not? Most of them are charmers, friendly to the customers and super appreciative of support. And they can play golf. There is a desperate echelon on the circuit hoping to break 80 each day, draw a check and keep them from retiring to a secretary's desk, but for the most part the field has a majority compliment of serious practitioners who constantly seek to improve. Janie Blalock, last year's rookie-of-the-year, claims she has crammed about six years of experience into her brief pro career already.

One time, Dick Taylor mentioned me and said, my off-course public relations did more in the early days for the tour than any amount of victories.

•

I carried a dictionary with me when I traveled, always on the lookout for unusual words. My all-time favorite is "indefatigable," an adjective that means untiring. I first heard it in Bermuda at a golf outing. A lady playing bridge with me used it and I filed it away as a pet word. (I'm laughing … because I just got to use it.)

•

Mary Mills had a 14-year old caddie named Stanley. Stanley had little experience but he worked hard and hustled like crazy. His real drawback was his poor eyesight; his glasses were like the bottom of a Coke bottle. It was raining and that didn't help, his glasses were wet so he had trouble seeing Mary's ball ... until he dropped the golf bag on it (add one stroke).

•

I was in a tournament at Glen Lakes Country Club in Dallas. There were two parallel holes, separated by a screen. I hit a shot, errant of course, that not only hit the screen, the ball went through and hit Peggy Wilson. In one year's time, Peggy was hit three times—twice by pro-am partners. Is that what they call target golf?

A stray cat ran up to Mary Lou Daniel Crocker when she was on the green and bit her in the leg.

Candy Phillips Anderson was locked inside a portable potty on the course.

Kathy Farrer was stung three times when she stepped on a wasp's nest.

•

In 1951, Shirley Spork was the first person to give exhibitions in Great Britain and France. At St. Andrews, after playing an 18-hole exhibition, she was the first lady pro to be invited into the clubhouse. She walked into the locker room and two men leaped out of their chairs. They never expected a woman to cross the threshold. Horrors.

•

In 1951, Shirley Spork became head professional at Ukiah Country Club in California. She was the second woman to become a head pro, Helen Dettweiler was the first. Shirley worked at Ukiah for two years.

She was proud of her accomplishments, but her responsibilities grew to the extent that the workload was a burden. She asked the club to hire an assistant. They declined. That did it. "Then you don't need me, either," she said … and she quit.

•

Barbara Romack—I affectionately nicknamed her Babo even though she was known as Little Tiger—joined the tour in 1959, and was regularly voted Best Dressed Woman Golfer of the year. Tommy Bolt was regularly voted Best Dressed Male Golfer.

Terrible Tommy couldn't stand it. He erupted, complaining, "She's not the best dressed, I am."

Not long after, they both happened to be on the practice range at the Haig & Haig Scotch Foursome Tournament. Barbara sidled up to him and said, "I'm curious, Tommy, do your undies match your clothes?"

•

In the early 1960s, Barbara did promotional work for MacGregor at a trade show in Chicago. Afterward, she was due to fly home to Palm Beach with a stopover in Tampa. At Tampa, a man brandishing a gun boarded the plane, entered the cockpit and told the pilot to take him to Havana.

The pilot got on the intercom and informed the passengers that there would be a little side trip to Cuba. Barbara said she rang for the stewardess, immediately, and ordered a scotch. The plane landed safely in Havana where a platoon of passengers bolted from the plane and made a mad dash to the bar. They ultimately made it to Palm Beach safely, but what a trip.

•

Barbara Romack took flying lessons. The airport in Sacramento was right next to a golf course. She said, "That made me comfortable when I landed. If I missed the runway, I knew I'd wind up on the course. My instructor said I'd probably get a bad lie. I told him with my luck I'd probably wind up in a bunker."

•

One time Judy Rankin's group was searching for her golf ball. "Here it is," her caddie exclaimed, "I found it, and it wasn't even out of bounds." Judy was relieved. "Thank heavens," she said, "Where is it?" The caddie grinned, proud of himself for saving Judy a penalty, and held out of his hand. Sure enough, there it was … in his hand.

•

On tour, we fined players for throwing clubs. If it hit the ground, the player owed the LPGA treasury $50. Jo Ann Prentice, a fireball from Alabama, missed a short putt one time and threw her club in the air. Realizing the consequences, she raced to catch it before it hit the ground. Turned out to be a free throw. Her favorite football team was the University of Alabama and we heard about it, nonstop—including the off-season.

•

In 1985, Mickey Wright and Kathy Whitworth played in the Liberty Mutual Legends of Golf Tournament, a better-ball event that was the beginning of the popular PGA Senior Tour.

The girls played against the boys from the back tees, and they drew a crowd. Between them they had won four U.S. Opens, seven LPGA Championships and 169 tournaments.

Kathy was still playing the LPGA tour, but Mickey had been retired for a decade and suffered from a nerve condition in her feet. Fortunately, the event permitted carts so she rode. It may have been Mickey's last competitive round.

The Wright-Whitworth team did well for themselves finishing 18th in a 28 team field.

Harvey Penick, the legendary teaching pro, was there. He told Kathy, "When you or Mickey hit a good shot I get goose bumps." That was high praise from a master of the game.

•

One rainy night, Betty Jameson walked in with water dripping off her visor, carrying her putter and chipping iron. "Where have you been?" inquired another player.

"Out putting and chipping," Betty said.

"But it's dark and raining."

Betty, smiling as though she had unlocked the secret to a perfect short game, replied, "It's light enough for me."

•

Another Betty Jameson exchange:

Babe Zaharias asked her, "Why don't you get a new car?" mentioning that new Oldsmobiles were available to the pros at factory prices.

"New car?" Betty replied. "I just got a new motor for my '48 Plymouth."

•

In the 1960s, a player had to be in the Top 15 on the money list in order to make expenses and put some money away. As a member of the Top 15, I got to drive a new Oldsmobile Tornado with my name and the LPGA logo on the doors. I remember a filling station attendant looking at the emblem and asking, "What circus are you with, lady?"

•

A note I wrote in 1975:

"I've gone back to my beloved aluminum shafted clubs. I know I won't start a stampede in the pro shops, but I must say these shafts have their place in golf. I find I minimize errors, feel less shock at impact and do get distance. I don't know why I put them away, because I've had some of my best years playing with alums. I would think that many players, both women and men, might find these shafts advantageous."

Question: Did you ever play with aluminum shafts? Didn't think so. Ever find a set in the attic? Manufacturers claimed they were the hottest new thing—much lighter than steel. The public didn't buy into it and the revolution was short lived. But they worked for me.

•

Look how they botched my hero's name.

> Miss Smith, who says she has a golf game with "Stan The Man" Musical in St. Louis Tuesday, also took time to shower praise on the LPGA's new top two officials — executive director Bud Erickson and tournament supervisor Ed Griffiths.

•

152

Many years ago I played golf at Hollywood Beach Golf Course in Florida where I met Joe Gerlack. Joe was a character. He owned a driving range across the street from Gulfstream Park. He said, "We could hear the races over the PA system. In fact, my assistant used to run over there and bet on the horses. Then he'd come back to give a lesson. If his horse lost, he'd slam the club on the ground—right in the middle of a lesson."

•

One time JoAnne Carner and Mickey Wright—both long hitters—were paired together. Before play, Mickey told JoAnne she didn't want to get into a long drive competition off the tees. Things went well for several holes until Mickey bombed a drive far past JoAnne's ball. That triggered an I-dare-you-to-beat-me driving contest—accuracy meant nothing. Their scores soared. Finally, Mickey came to her senses. She offered to play closest to the pin for a penny-a-hole. JoAnne said, "Why didn't you say that in the first place?"

•

The 1960 Titleholders week started out with a surprise snowfall and enough accumulation for Jo Ann Prentice, Mickey Wright and Betsy Rawls to make a five-foot snowman. Pedestrians and people in passing cars did a double take when they saw it. As if that wasn't enough, the players had a snowball fight. Mickey, Betsy and Louise Suggs even found a sled and went sled riding. The tournament was just delayed one day, but playing in the snow was more fun than getting blisters on the practice range.

Bad Weather and Tough Courses

In 1950, the Weathervane Tournament was played at Skycrest Country Club in Chicago. The weather plays tricks in Chicago. That particular day it treated us to 60-mph winds. I was paired with Louise Suggs and Shirley Spork. Shirley tried to hit a three-wood but the wind blew her off balance and she missed the ball. Shirley and I thought it was knee-slapping funny.

Louise was amazing. She shot 78 that day. I still remember it as one of the best rounds I ever witnessed.

In 1967, we played the 6,950-yard Monster Golf Course at The Concord at Kiamesha, New York. It was monstrous, all right. For added fun it rained all week. Shirley "Dimples" Englehorn found magic in her one-iron. It was her secret weapon. She used it off the tees to escape casual water in the fairways and more often than not her approach shot landed pin high. She scored 77-76-76—quite a feat from the back tees under miserable conditions.

The Monster was the toughest course of all. The course superintendent didn't have to trick it up; the layout, itself, was brutal. It took finesse out of the game. Tommy Armour, the Silver Scot, described Oakmont as "muscle-tightening terror." He could just as well have been talking about the Monster.

PS: These days, the Monster stretches out to 7,650-yards and it's still par 72

The shortest course I recall playing was Lake Worth Golf Club during the 1960 Lake Worth Open in Florida. It measured a mere 5,900 yards but the ocean breeze and thick, grainy Bermuda greens made play almost impossible. Thankfully, I have no idea what I shot.

My Family

My dad's name was Owen Lynn Smith. L-Y-N-N. That's how I got the name Marilynn—with two Ns. All through my career, and to this day, people forget or miss the second N. I have cartons of articles and clippings and close to half of them have my name spelled wrong. Columnists and reporters wrote stories about me, flattering stories in many cases, with a headline—*a headline*—that said Marilyn Smith, and the entire article followed suit. Having two Ns in my name is distinctive ... well, most of the time.

My mother, Alma, was born in Germany and lived there for a short time. Her mother, my grandmother Lillian, married a German. His family gave him grief about his wife being an American, so they packed up and came to the United States.

Unfortunately, during World War II, young kids in our neighborhood in Wichita found out she came from Germany and threw stones at her bedroom window. That was a difficult time.

My mother was a fine homemaker, she loved to knit, play bridge, garden and draw cartoons. She was a nine-hole golfer and enjoyed traveling with me on some of my Spalding exhibition tours—often picking up tips that helped her own golf game. My dad was a quiet, thoughtful, honest person. He was the general agent for Connecticut Mutual Life Insurance Company in Kansas. It was fun going with him when he visited clients in nearby cities. We were both people watchers so he'd park the car where we could watch people go by.

My parents lived by the Golden Rule and taught my sister, Gay, and me to do the same.

My mother's meals were the fuel that kept me active. When I was young it was common for families to eat certain foods on certain days—week in and week out. In our case, Sunday was chicken day. We should have invited Colonel Sanders over for dinner. KFC might have paid a fortune for my mother's fried chicken and dumplings recipe, or her stewed chicken and noodles recipe.

I didn't cook much growing up, but I sure washed a lot of dishes. As it turned out, I was always on the move during my career, living in hotels and motels, so culinary skills weren't important.

My kid sister, Gay, is 12 years younger. She heard so much about golf from my dad and me that she took up swimming. I remember the time I asked how she had done in a swimming meet. She said, "I came in third." I asked how many were in the race and she said, three. You know, I was proud that she said she finished third, not last.

Gay and her husband, Clifford Pappas, were high school sweethearts and both attended Kansas State University. They had two children, Michele and Marilynn. Clifford has a doctorate in food science and works for the American Institute of Baking. They live nearby in Arizona and we keep tabs on each other, every day.

When my grandmother, Lillian, was young she studied to be a concert pianist. I guess there was a trickle down effect because years later my mother wanted me to play the piano. That meant practicing—and I took lessons from age six to seventeen—for at least an hour every day after school. I must say I had a super rendition of "Malaguena" (at least I thought so). The problem was my performance wasn't meant for the stage. In the middle of a piano recital, I totally blanked out. All I could do was apologize as I walked off the stage.

I was a good student, even served on student council at East High School in Wichita, but once the bell rang I was out the door like I had been launched. If I wasn't playing baseball I was playing golf, or kick the can. Just thinking about all that energy makes me want to take a nap.

I attended the University of Kansas for two years before I turned pro and started touring. My studies took a back seat to golf, but I was elected president of the sophomore class.

•

A few years after I joined the tour, my dad and I played an exhibition match at Crestview Country Club against Judy Bell and her dad. At the time, we may have been the youngest girls to win a state championship (I won mine when I was 17, Judy was 15 when she won hers).

Dave Truffelli, the home pro, and others said they couldn't recall a match with two state champions partnered by fathers strong enough to play an exhibition.

The best part was my dad decided the outcome when he made par on No. 17 to put us one-up, and another par on No. 18 to hold the lead.

Adventures on the Road

In 1948 my Wichita golf pro, Mike Murra, drove me to Pebble Beach in my mother's Mercury to play in the National Amateur. Tires had inner tubes that punctured easily, lost air pressure and went flat. It was common. We had flat tires along the way—all four, in fact. It's a good thing Mike was there to fix them. I won a few matches in the Amateur, but ultimately lost.

One afternoon on that trip, Louise Suggs played golf with Bing Crosby at Cypress Point. I thought it would be fun to watch them. I went to the first tee to meet Bing with a can of cookies and offered him one. He said, "No thanks." I said, "Please, have a cookie." He opened the can and out popped a jack-in-the-box. I can't believe I did that, but we became good friends. He wrote me letters, encouraging me to play well. A couple years later, I played in the Bing Crosby Tournament in Guadalajara, Mexico.

Several Crosby stories come to mind. Shirley Spork and I were playing a practice round at Pebble Beach during a Handmacher Weathervane Tour stop and we ran into Bing at the ninth hole. He joined us for a few holes, but it began to rain so he invited us to his house. His den was fascinating. Wurlitzer built a custom record player—it was three-shelves high. Bing selected a record and a mechanical arm went up the shelves, got the record, placed it on the turntable and, voila! Music. Guess what—there weren't any Crosby recordings in the collection. None. (Why in the world didn't I ask him to sing for us? Boy, did I bogey that one.) When the rain let up, he drove us back to the pro shop. Bing had a carriage bell mounted on his floorboard and he rang us into the parking area—like a police escort. Before long, Shirley and I had carriage bells in our cars, too.

My grandmother, Lillian Fogg traveled with me for a while in California when I was giving Spalding golf clinics. One day, at Pebble Beach, the Spalding salesman took us to the pro shop to meet the pro and Bing happened to be in the shop. My grandmother, the pistol that she was, said, "Mr. Crosby, I've always wanted to be on a radio quiz show. Can you get me on one of them?" Indeed, he could.

"Double or Nothing" on CBS radio, hosted by Walter O'Keefe, booked her. She was delighted. We went to the studio to tape the show. They gave her four warm up questions they'd ask after they introduced her on the program. She only had a moment to read them before the interview started. O'Keefe welcomed her and asked, "Why are you in California?" She said, "I'm traveling with my granddaughter. She's a pro. You know, she works for one of those sporting houses." The audience went wild. She added, "My other daughter is married to the Governor of Kansas so I'm just thrilled up and down both sides." When calm was restored, she answered all four questions and won a beautiful gold watch.

After the show, we ran out of gas in the desert and I had to walk to a gas station wearing a brown suit and high heels. It was only about a half-mile (call it a par-5 and a par-4). I got back to the car in time to hear the taped program. They edited the show's highlight, where she said I worked for one of those sporting houses. Thank goodness.

My grandmother enjoyed being with the golfers and they enjoyed having her around. She liked to sit on the floor and shoot craps with Marlene Hagge and Sybil Griffin. I come from good stock.

•

I conducted a Spalding golf clinic at the Grumman Aircraft Company, on Long Island. A gentleman told me that he heard I had never been on an airplane. "That's right," I said, "I'm afraid to fly." He said, "I'm a pilot. I'll take you up in a plane after the clinic." I thought he was kidding, which was a good thing—had I known he was serious I wouldn't have been able to take the club back during my clinic. Either that, or I would have skipped town. Sure enough, he was waiting after the clinic. "Let's go," he said. I have no idea how I managed to get in the plane. We took off, flew for a few minutes and landed in the water. How was I to know it was an amphibious plane? There's nothing like finishing your maiden flight with a pilot who thinks he's Sully Sullenberger.

•

My first commercial flight was on American Airlines from New York to Boston. It was cloudy as we were about to land but I saw a gap in the clouds and thought the pilot would go through it. Technology wasn't what it is today so we had to veer off and my first commercial flight ended with a surprise finish. We landed in Vermont. *Vermont.* It was a seven-hour bus trip back to Boston. I liked American Airlines after that because I felt they were most interested in passenger safety. I didn't care much for the bus ride, though.

•

Shirley Spork, the first female club pro at the Tamarisk Country Club, gave lessons to several notables, including Walter Annenberg, the media tycoon and philanthropist. "He was left-handed," she said, "and he looped the club at the top of his swing. Whenever I saw him I'd say, 'Hey there, Zorro.'"

•

When we played Tamarisk in Palm Springs, Dolores Hope invited Shirley and me to dinner at the tennis club. I remember driving down Palm Canyon Drive, the street that's lined with spectacular lighted palm trees. Wow! It was the first of many times with Dolores. She is an honorary LPGA member. In 2008, she gave the LPGA Foundation $1 million to help former players who need financial assistance. She was also a generous contributor to my Marilynn Smith Scholarship Fund.

•

In 1955, I finished runner-up to Babe Zaharias in the Betsy Rawls Peach Blossom Tournament in Spartanburg, South Carolina. I was 2-strokes up at the turn but the back nine was a different story. Too many "Please hand me my sand-wedge" caddie requests. It was Babe's last tournament victory, which made it memorable.

•

After she won her first LPGA victory in the 1956 St. Petersburg Women's Open, Kathy Cornelius' LPGA competitors tossed her in Sunset Country Club swimming pool. She didn't see it coming, but took it like a good sport. In 1958, Bonnie Randolph got dunked when she won her first victory, the Heart-of-America tournament in Kansas City.

Marilynn Smith

•

Wiffi Smith played the piano—in her Volkswagen Microbus. Honest, she drove around with a piano. She played it to strengthen her fingers and wrists for better club control. After her career was cut short the players missed the way she powered her way around a golf course, her uninhibited nature and infectious personality.

•

In 1958, I lived in Tequesta, Florida. Perry Como's house was about a half-mile up the road. One day he asked me to join him in a round of golf. "If I win," he said, "you give me a dozen golf balls. If you win, I'll give you some Kraft cheese," (his television show was sponsored by Kraft Foods). The pro won. Two weeks later, a case of Kraft cheese showed up.

•

In 1960, the Muskogee, Oklahoma newspaper ran this item:

Golf star Carol Mann suggests a player with the beauty of Raquel Welch, links skills of Mickey Wright and the personality of Marilynn Smith as the ideal woman golfer needed to boost attendance and generate more interest.

•

When Shirley Spork and I traveled together on tour, we went to Catholic mass every Sunday. I'm not Catholic and she knew it, but it was never a problem. One Sunday I said, "Let's go to a Congregational Church." Months went by. A group of us were passing time, you know, sitting around talking about politics and life in general. The conversation got around to religion and I said, "Hey, Shirley how did you like going to a Protestant church?" She gave me a look, "Marilynn," she said, "it all depends if you want to go to heaven in a Ford or a Cadillac."

•

A bridge led from the sixteenth green to the seventeenth tee at a tournament in Mt. Clemens, Michigan. Jo Ann Prentice was on the bridge—along with a number of spectators—when it collapsed. She wound up in three-feet of water. Jo Ann climbed out, squished her way to the next tee and started to take her shoes off. But the tournament director wasn't having any. "No time for that," he said. "Play on, we're on TV." For Jo Ann, the final two holes were water holes.

Gallery Etiquette, Before "You 'da Man"

From the 1971 Len Immke Buick Open program

This is the players' competition. Treat them, as you would like to be treated.

Be silent and motionless when a player takes a stance and throughout the stroke.

Give the players plenty of room.

Walk; never run.

Avoid applause until merited. Do not make it obvious if you favor one player over another. Do not applaud just as another stroke is being made.

Be fair to players without galleries.

Stay behind the ropes and white lines.

Never run across a fairway. Keep your head up. Do not wander aimlessly.

Do not call "Down in front."

Walk around traps and bunkers, never through them.

Walk around greens, never over them.

Ladies should wear sport shoes.

If the gallery is large, kneel if you are in front.

Always have your ticket conspicuous.

The marshals are your friends. Please cooperate.

I don't know who wrote this, but ***"You 'da man!"***

Letters and Memories

I received this letter 30 years after Gayle Runke, a 16-year old girl, played in my pro-am group. It came out of the blue. I had no idea that she pursued a golf career.

Dear Marilynn,

Often I have reflected back on that week and the impact it has had on my golfing career. THANK YOU for being the example that you were, to me, and many others.

You set a terrific example, for me, and thousands of other young girls teaching us how to play the game and conduct oneself on and off the course. Thank you for taking the extra time and effort to make a young girl feel special and teaching her a few lessons that have lasted a lifetime.

Gayle Runke, Golf Coach
Southwest Missouri State University
Springfield, MO

•

Renee Powell, former LPGA player; currently head pro at Clearview Golf Club in East Canton, Ohio:

I was only 12 years old when my parents took me to my first LPGA event—a tournament in Alliance, Ohio not far from my hometown, East Canton.

Until that time, I had no idea there were lady professional golfers, but I soon found out differently.

As we walked on the golf course I spotted a lady wearing a beautiful powder blue knit skirt with a matching top, pearl earrings and a pearl necklace around her neck. She topped it off with a white straw hat. She looked like she had just stepped out of a model magazine.

When she looked my way she gave a little wave and instantly became my favorite player. The next two days my parents took me back to the tournament and I only wanted to follow the lady with the pearls, Marilynn Smith.

At the end of the tournament I waited for her to sign her scorecard and then she walked over to me gave me an autographed golf ball and asked for my address.

Meeting Marilynn Smith inspired me to want to become an LPGA Tour player and have my name on my bag, too. As an amateur I began playing Spalding golf clubs and even asked Spalding to stamp Marilynn Smith on my Spalding Executive clubs.

When I joined the Tour nearly 10 years later, I already had one good friend who just happens to be one of the Founding Members of the LPGA.

Renee

•

This letter of support—from George Dawson, vice president of Spalding—meant the world to me.

March 13, 1958

Dear Marilynn.

Congratulations! It couldn't have happened to a nicer person.

I've been delighted with the fine golf you have played in all the tournaments so far this year. And I've been expecting you to crash through at any time, but don't you think your spectacular chip shot on the last hole was a bit too rough on your pal Fay (Crocker)? Now that you apparently have developed the competitive concentration to go with your fine game, I hope you will be the big winner all year. Your many ardent admirers, of which I am one, will be eagerly watching for you to take your rightful place at the top of the LPGA.

Best wishes for your continued success.

George Dawson

173

Marilynn Smith

BEN HOGAN   P.O. Box 11276   Ft. Worth, Texas 76110

Dear Marilynn:

Please accept my congratulations on your being selected one of the Charter Members inducted into Kansas Golf Hall of Fame at Prairie Dunes Country Club in Hutchison, Kansas on Monday, September 30, 1991.

I am pleased that you have been so honored — a recognition which is greatly deserved for all you have given to the game we love so much.

I am also pleased to have had the opportunity to know you; so let's turn the clock back and start all over again.

Again, my heartiest congratulations to you, and with very best wishes, I am

Sincerely

Ben

October 17, 1991

Marilynn Smith

World Golf Hall of Fame member, Amy Alcott:

"Your unique and genuine personality was a real model for me in my early years on the tour. I remember Marilynn in her skirts, smiling and waving to people ... good shot or bad. Your special appeal was what the LPGA was all about. Thank you for being such a beacon of light to a young 19-year old with big aspirations."

•

Nan Ryan, the LPGA director of public relations in the 1960s:

"I first met Marilynn when she came to my hometown Quincy, Illinois to give exhibitions. I was a teenager and she asked me to hit balls during the clinic. A year later, she picked me out of an LPGA tournament gallery and invited me to walk with her. During my senior year in college she invited me to participate in clinics. I jumped at the chance.

"One day we were crossing the street in Ft. Worth when she shook hands with a man, and said, "Ben, this is Nan Ryan.' My knees buckled—it was Ben Hogan.

"In restaurants, she stopped at tables to talk to complete strangers. By the time the food was served, she was on a first-name basis with people at several tables around us.

175

"She has a uncanny ability to meet and REMEMBER people—not just their names, but important things about them. My travels and experiences with Marilynn helped shape my life work as founder and executive director of the International Pepsi Titan Little People's Golf Championships."

•

Betsy Rawls, first four-time winner of the U.S. Women's Open:

"As president of the LPGA in the early 60's, I was always concerned about keeping the sponsors that we had and also increasing the number of tournaments on the schedule.

"We were able to have a reasonably good schedule because people liked the players and enjoyed having them in town for a week.

"My job of helping maintain good relationships with sponsors was made easier by the great public relations job done by the tour players.

"The shining example of these efforts was Marilynn Smith. Her friendliness and warmth toward people—sponsors, volunteers, spectators, local press, and everyone involved in putting on an event—helped tremendously to endear the LPGA to our fans and supporters. Marilynn gave the LPGA a valuable boost in appreciation and respect."

•

Sandra Post, the first Canadian golfer to play the LPGA tour and winner of the 1968 LPGA Championship:

"Marilynn wore a mid-calf straight skirt, matching sweater sets and pearls. She had a huge red and white Spalding golf bag with her distinctive autographed name on the side. She waved to spectators continuously and they cheered back.

"I was five-years old in 1953 when I first saw her at an LPGA event in St. Petersburg, Florida. I must have caught her eye because before I knew it, I was sitting on her golf bag watching her practice.

"When I was seven, I told her I would be with her on tour one day. She patted my head and told me to practice. I wrote to her throughout the year and told her of my accomplishments and she always wrote back, with congratulations. Fourteen years after I met Marilynn in 1968, I joined her on tour. I too, had a big red bag and a contract from Spalding, thanks to Marilynn. There is no question my parents gave me the opportunity to play and eventually join the tour—but Marilynn was the light. I caught the spark she threw off in 1953, and never looked back."

Marilynn Smith

•

Susie Maxwell Berning, three-time U.S. Women's Open champion:

"When I was a rookie on tour—and without much amateur experience—I felt lost in an unknown environment. I was fortunate that Marilynn Smith was there. She and a few others made me feel part of the tour and took time out of their busy schedules to show me the ropes.

"Marilynn, you made life enjoyable for the players and gallery. You and your founding partners gave those of us who followed a livelihood."

•

Jane Crafter, former LPGA player; now an announcer for Golf Channel, NBC and ESPN:

"I met Marilynn when I was 16-years old. I had to go to school that day, but after school I made it to the course with my mother and brother. At the time I was a good junior golfer and played in several Adelaide, Australia junior tournaments. Marilynn let me caddie the last few holes. I was a good junior golfer and when the exhibition ended Marilynn said, "Why don't I watch you hit a few balls on the range?" She did, and that was a wonderful experience for me. She was encouraging and complimentary about my golf swing and that gave me a lot of confidence to continue with my aspirations for a golf career."

•

I'm always happy to pass on my life lessons to youngsters. It is a privilege. In this case, a father asked me to write to his son.

Dear Nick,

Your father has asked me to write to you regarding some principles I feel are important in life.

Do your best! Try to do your best in everything you do whether it is trying to sink a three-foot putt or trying to figure out a math problem. (Remember, Einstein failed math.) Math and Science teach us how to think. Think "Math is beautiful!" Do your best and you will be happy. You cannot fail. You can accomplish almost everything you want if you are willing to work at it. ENJOY!

Honesty! Do not cheat on tests or on the golf course. It's OK to make mistakes; we all do, so own up to them and try not to make the same mistake again. One does not have to win a tournament to be a WINNER in life.

Be Happy! No one wants to be around a grump. Be gracious in winning or losing on the golf course, just as you would be gracious if you win or lose in a Spelling Bee competition.

Patience! Have patience with yourself and with others. If some one doesn't learn as fast as you, have patience with them

Parents! Feel comfortable in telling your parents how you feel about golf. Some youngsters don't want to be pushed into playing golf, or playing as well as their parents would like them to play. Kids are people, too, and have a right to express themselves. Help your parents understand your feelings.

Find something that is special to you! Each of us can make a difference and contribute to society.

Golden Rule! My father told me as a youngster to follow the Golden Rule.

Remember to be all the person you can be! Be thankful for what you have – Family, Friends, God and Teachers.

Nick, you are one lucky fella to have the parents you have. God bless you and your mother and father.

Warm regards,

Marilynn Smith

Good, Not So Good and Wow!

Good

In the 1960s the Shell Oil Company sponsored televised golf matches called "Shell's Wonderful World of Golf." Gene Sarazen, who hosted the series, was the first golfer to win all four major professional titles. I think his presence and demeanor gave the series credibility. Now and then, the matches are seen on Golf Channel. It's nice that the younger generation can watch the 'old-timers' in action. They can see what golf was like back then and appreciate how far the game has come with modern teaching techniques, equipment upgrades and course conditioning. Add to that, many matches were filmed in black and white movie film as compared to the extraordinary video coverage we enjoy today.

Shell Oil was known globally so they scheduled several matches at foreign courses. Sometimes an American competed against an international player. It added interest and gave the show a broader dimension. Top amateurs participated, as well. It took a few years, but Shell included women's matches, giving the LPGA valuable exposure.

Mickey Wright played Marlene Streit at Toronto G.C.; Mickey also played Brigette Varangot at Estoril G.C. in Portugal. Carol

Mann and Sandra Haynie played at Lausanne, Switzerland. Sandra Haynie, Carol Mann and Kathy Whitworth played together at The Royal Bangkok Sports Club in Thailand. I defeated Marley Spearman, the English Amateur Champion at Luxembourg G.C. and lost to Canadian Marlene Stewart Streit at Oslo Golfklubb in Norway. Barbara Romack defeated Isa Goldschmidt, the Italian champion, at Monaco G.C.

It snowed the week before my match in Oslo. The greens were in bad shape but Marlene putted exceptionally well. We waited a long time between shots—cameras had to be moved and repositioned. As such, it was not unusual for an 18-hole match to be filmed over two days.

Did you know that Gene Sarazan changed his name from Eugenio Saraceni? He said Saraceni sounded more like a violin player. Just thought I'd pass on a bit of interesting trivia.

•

The Waterloo Women's Open Invitational at Sunnyside Country Club in Waterloo, Iowa was one of our best early events. The tournament showcased the city, population 70,000. Marion Lichty and other Sunnyside members attempted to secure corporate sponsors for the tournament but it was difficult task. So the club had to cover all expenses—and they did. They even footed the bill for a banquet.

With all that, they made a $7,000 profit and used the money to help build a new clubhouse. Hooray for Waterloo and Sunnyside.

Amateurs contributed to the purse to play in the pro-am—and it was sold out. Fay Crocker won the first year, in a 19-player field. The LPGA could only afford to pay 18 places, so gallery members passed a hat and raised $50 for Gloria Fecht who finished in last place. How's that for generosity?

Sunnyside Country Club members housed several players, including our families and pets. They also babysat children—and a dog, or two—in the ladies' locker room. They bought dinner for the players, our families and friends. Even today, some players remain close to the host families. A local radio station broadcast from No. 18 during the final round. The turnout was so large you had to wonder if anybody stayed home to listen.

Not So Good

Sandra Palmer and I were playing a par-3 at the Colgate-Dinah Shore one time when my tee shot landed in a greenside bunker. I played an explosion shot on to the green, marked the ball and gave it to the caddie to clean. When it was my turn to putt I asked him for the ball. He said, "I don't have it." I said, "You don't have it? I don't have it, where is it? Look in your pocket." He did. "I don't have it," he said, "I can't find it." He searched, but no ball. I had to declare a lost ball—*on the green*, of all places—and take a penalty. Caddies used to bet, which may have had something to do with the vanishing act. If that was the case he probably cashed in because I missed the cut. Sandra said I should have fired him on the spot. Maybe, but without proof?

•

It's interesting to compare different sports to golf. For instance, a batter facing a pitcher who throws 100 mph fastballs amid 50,000 screaming fans, compared to a golfer standing over a three-foot putt surrounded by 3,000 dead-silent spectators. I mention the comparison because I was on the green one time paired with a player who shall remain nameless. As I stepped up to address a 10-foot putt she started humming. Well, I thought, she must not know I'm getting ready to putt. Maybe she's staring at something in the distance. I backed away, waited and addressed the ball again. More humming. Gamesmanship. I knew she was trying to distract me. It worked, the putt lipped-out. But there is a golf god—she missed her putt, too. On the way to the next tee she put her arm around me and said, "I'm so sorry we both missed our putts." I was upset and started to cry. The tournament director told me later, "Don't worry about it, we know all about her."

•

One time in a tournament at the Homestead, rain came down in torrents. When play began, the cup on the first hole was filled with water, to the brim. One player stuck a towel in the cup to absorb the water. Then she putted out. When she finished she squeezed the water from the towel back in the cup and replaced the pin. Can you believe that?

•

Back in the 1950s, I was invited to conduct an indoor clinic for patients at the Menninger Psychiatric Hospital in Topeka, Kansas. Twelve patients stood in a line, but one faced the wall. I was at a loss to understand or explain why. He stood that way throughout my 30-minute presentation. The image remains with me, some 60 years later.

•

There was a rules sheet mix-up at the Shreveport Kiwanis Invitational Golf Tournament. The rules sheet said "preferred lies" which I interpreted as improve your lie on the fairway, and I did.

Oops, the rule only applied to the amateurs in the group. My team played beautifully, but the officials penalized us two-strokes.

•

I was paired with Anne Murray, the Grammy Award winning singer from Canada in the Dinah Shore pro-am. She was just learning the game so I gave her the five-hour version of Golf-101. By the time we finished I was ready to take up hockey.

Wow!

In 1963, I had my first competitive hole-in-one playing with Marlene Hagge on No. 11 at Glen Lakes Country Club in Dallas. I hit a three-iron that barely got off the ground—a laser shot, no more than eight-feet high. Marlene rolled her eyes. She thought it was a fluke. Fluke? I was aiming at the hole all the way.

•

I had two double eagles during my career. In 1971, I was paired with Carol Mann when I made the first double eagle in LPGA history at the Lady Carling Open at Pine Ridge Golf Course in Baltimore. We were on No. 1, a 485-yard, par-five. I hit a four-wood into the hole. A good gentleman friend in the gallery perched on a shooting stick fell over from astonishment—or maybe it was shock.

There was no way to prove it, but I never heard of a double eagle on the first hole of any golf course.

The icing on the cake was Carol Mann hitting a perfect four-iron on the 171-yard, par-3 eighth hole for a hole-in-one. We really put on a show for the gallery that day.

•

I made my second double-eagle in New Zealand. I hit a long drive on a par-5, 500-yard hole with a dogleg left. For my second shot, I had to hook a three-wood around a huge grove of trees, and I pulled it off. There were only two people at the green but they started yelling, "The ball went in the hole. The ball went in the hole!" I couldn't see it, I was behind the trees but their excitement was enough to let me know I had holed-out.

Not In This Century, You Don't

Babe Zaharias was to the LPGA what Arnold Palmer was to the PGA Tour. She made people pay attention. She became the face of the LPGA. When she stepped on the first tee, the rest of the field wondered where the gallery had gone.

Decades after Babe holed her final putt, 1987 to be exact, I established the Marilynn Smith Founders' Classic, the first senior women's professional tournament. It was meant to honor the LPGA founders.

Before I tell you about it, I want to share a piece Betty Hicks wrote at that time. She didn't mince words:

•

NOT IN THIS CENTURY, YOU DON'T!

By, Betty Hicks

If Babe Zaharias were alive today, would there be an LPGA Senior Tour?

If Babe Zaharias were alive today, she'd be thrusting her 75-year-old forefinger in Marilynn Smith's face, demanding, "Put those tees back for your Founders' Classic, or I don't play. And then see where you're gonna get your galleries."

If Babe Zaharias were alive today, she would stomp into the office of the president of Wilson Sporting Goods Company, ordaining the retention of her personal manager to set up an LPGA Senior Tour. "Need to win me some tournaments," she'd protest, "not just play exhibitions." Patently déjà vu!

But there would probably be an LPGA Senior Tour, starring 20 contestants straining to conquer shabbily groomed 6,700-yard golf courses in 18 tournaments a year. Prize money would be miniscule.

But Babe Zaharias died in 1956, an irreplaceable marquee monopolizer in the show biz of competitive golf. So there will be no LPGA Senior Tour in this 20th century, unless one or two or three tournaments may be glorified by the name "Tour."

Various administrators and seers of women's golf have highlighted the reasons for this mournful forecast:

"You are simply not marketable," wrote a former LPGA official to one of us in response to her request to promote women's senior events. "You haven't had enough TV exposure."

"There aren't enough of you seniors," observed a top LPGA star.

The oft-whispered reality is that sponsor money does not extend to infinity. With the PGA, the LPGA, and the PGA Seniors Tour slurping at the corporate troughs, there's little room for the runt of the litter, the LPGA Seniors Tour. That Marilynn Smith has put together one moneyed event is tribute to the extraordinary perseverance and acumen of a diligent and talented woman and a corps of volunteers assembled around the energy field of her charisma.

And we ashamedly confess there *weren't* enough of us in those days of our early struggles, because the LPGA was conceived in an era in which it was not considered proper for women to compete for money in sports. The LPGA was launched only nine years after famed Atlanta golf writer O.B. Keeler had bemoaned the demise of truly feminine golfers with his *Atlanta Journal* story headlined, "Ladylike Golf Victors? They're Gone Now." Many parents, along with influential women's amateur golf officials warned young women that the LPGA tour was not a wholesome environment in which a young woman should live and work. The young WPGA/LPGA coaxed in vain to lure greater numbers of outstanding amateurs into the play-for-pay arena.

Television was a mere toddler when the LPGA was chartered in 1950. We did not appear on the tube until the 1961 LPGA Championship in Las Vegas. None of us became household names as a consequence of this furtive exposure. No, we probably aren't marketable.

Another factor contributing to our deficient numbers is our dropout rate. With a handful of notable exceptions, professionals retiring from the LPGA tour have but one destination--the lesson tee. How do teaching professionals keep their games tuned for the occasional tournament appearances? They don't. To protect their egos they elect not to play tournaments. The number of non-competing seniors who otherwise enjoyed the festivities at the 1987 Marilynn Smith Founders' Classic was adequate to comprise a separate Hall-of-Fame-class event!

The 20th century, a mere decade of it remaining, will *not* feature an LPGA Senior Tour. Cherish the illusion, baby, that we've come a long way.

•

As far as I was concerned, the Marilynn Smith Founders' Classic made sense. (If you've read this far you know I don't give up easily.) Andy Bell, of the Chilton Foundation, contacted me with the idea of a women's senior professional tournament and asked if I could get it going. The idea caught on at a men's Senior Tour event at Bent Tree Country Club in Dallas. When I pitched the concept to a group of men at the practice range Jerry Johansen's eyes lit up. "Count me in," he said.

Amazing. It was like a one-round knockout. I didn't even know Jerry; it was the first time we'd met. He was co-owner and chief executive at Ginnie Johansen Designs, specializing in women's accessories and perfume. "Marilynn is one of the most positively enthusiastic people you could ever meet," he said. "She has a genuineness about her that's hard to resist. Without that sense of fun, without that positive enthusiasm, we wouldn't have this tournament."

We had our general chairman.

Big business jumped on the bandwagon. Campbell Soup, Dr. Pepper, Ford Motor, Frito-Lay, Nabisco, Interstate Battery System of Dallas, Haggar Foundation, PPA Industries and M/A/R/C participated—evidence that more than 40 former players still had drawing power. We raised $400,000 and donated $50,000 to Excel Charities in Dallas. The money benefited deaf and retarded children in four charities: Callier Center for Communication Disorders, Helping Hand Development Center, Notre Dame Special School and Vocational Center, and the Special Care and Career Center.

The message was clear: "Through Excel Charities, we can reach out for a special child and we can make their world a better place."

I met the president of Ford at a golf tournament in Dayton and the vice president of Campbell Soup during a trip to Hawaii. Those contacts helped. I also solicited my friends. Four of them donated $10,000 apiece. There's an old saying: It's not what you know it's whom you know.

Ben and Valerie Hogan came to the pre-tournament dinner. When he walked in it was amazing—a hush came over the room. Ben charmed the crowd as he presented maroon blazers (with his name on the inside label) to each of the $10,000 sponsors and the nine surviving LPGA co-founders.

Byron and Peggy Nelson presented the awards to pro-am winners. Dolores Hope and Diana "Mousie" Powell flew in from Palm Springs as our special guests.

A newspaper clipping reminds me about some of the silent auction items. All these years later, they seem remarkably generous. There were vacations that golfers dream about; lunch with Arnold Palmer; golf, airfare and accommodations at Bay Hill; a week in the home of golf architects Alice and Pete Dye in the Dominican Republic; golf with Marlene Bauer Hagge and golf in Buenos Aires with Roberto DeVincenzo. The donors really stepped up to the plate.

Six of the nine surviving founders played in the three-day pro-am. The 1987 purse was $200,000 and Kathy Whitworth was the winner. Susie Maxwell Berning won in 1988, and Sandra Palmer in 1989. The first two tournaments were played at Las Colinas Country Club in Irving, the third at Prestonwood Country Club in Dallas.

Louise Suggs said, "Last month I hit Medicare, I have had a career that most people dream about. It's a great thing for women seniors to have their own tournament. My muscles have gone and my mind's not working any more but that's the aging process." (Then she went out and tied for second in the Grande Dames Tournament.)

Betty Hicks was wowed: "Nobody but Marilynn could do it. Nobody but Marilynn had those contacts."

Helen Dettweiler added, "Marilynn meant so much for golf in so many different ways, it's only natural she should have organized a tournament. I think her goodwill made more of an impression than her actual golf."

Fred Raphael, who started the Legends of Golf in Austin, told me it was the best first-year tournament he had ever seen. The accolades were nice, but I knew the second year would be the toughest. If you can get past the second year you're really rolling.

195

The trouble was our mid-October scheduling competed with two PGA Tour events, a Senior PGA Tour event, college football and the NFL—all in the same market. It was impossible to draw a substantial gallery.

Contributions remained about the same but a few sponsors pulled out, most notably Ford after they offered cars as par-3 hole-in-one prizes and two golfers drove home in a new Ford. Other sponsors cut back on their involvement. On the plus side, Karsten Solheim, head of Karsten Manufacturing upped his contribution from $10,000 to $25,000 and donated two of his four pro-am spots to the winner and runner-up of the Women's Western Senior Championship.

Before the second tournament, I announced, "We're not trying to start a Senior Tour for the ladies. We're just trying to lay a foundation. If it turns into a springboard for something else, that's great."

My Founders' Classic broke the ice, but it was a bit premature. As time went on, the PGA Senior Tour gained popularity. Golf fans enjoyed seeing the once popular tour players come back for an encore. They still attracted a crowd, and had fun doing it. For some, it was a new lease on life.

In my opinion, the time was right for the ladies to have another go at it in 2000. That's when Jane Blalock organized the first two Legends tour tournaments. At first, the players chipped in their own money to get the tour off the ground.

In June 2000, 26 lady pros competed in the HyVee Classic at the Hyperion Field Club in Johnston, Iowa. Jan Stephenson won the $35,000 first prize with a 3-under total. In August, Vicki Fergon's 10-under par score was worth $75,000 at the Shopko Great Lakes Classic played at Green Bay Country Club in Green Bay, Wisconsin.

The Legends tour has grown to 12 events on the 2012 schedule. Over $11 million has been raised for charity. Although the players are retired from the regular tour, they are amazing shot-makers and well worth the price of admission.

David Foster, the Man Who Introduced Us to America

David Foster will always be in my Hall of Fame; he appreciated the marketing connection between Colgate and the LPGA and he knew how grateful we were.

In 1989, I asked him to write something for the Marilynn Smith Founders' Classic. This was his reply:

"I was delighted when, during this year's Dinah Shore, a familiar face appeared over the privet hedge that guards our patio facing the lake at the sixth hole. Marilynn Smith had sought me out to ask if I would write a column to appear in the program of the third annual Marilynn Smith Founders' Classic to be held in October at Prestonwood Country Club, N. Dallas. The 1987 inaugural event, first women's senior tournament attracted 44 entries. The Lady Masters—Pros 45-54 play a 54-hole Medal Tournament, while the Grande Dames—Pros 55+ play a 36-hole team match. $50,000 was raised to help mentally retarded and deaf children.

"Marilynn, there is nothing that would give me greater pleasure because if it hadn't been for the support the players gave to us at

Colgate in those early days, there probably wouldn't be a major LPGA Championship at Mission Hills today.

"Sometime ago, when in a TV interview, I was asked the question as to why the Colgate-Dinah Shore had proved to be so successful I replied, without hesitation, that it was mainly due to the enthusiasm, cooperation and support given to it by the players themselves. All those eligible to play in that historic 1972 inaugural event entered, although illness forced two contestants to withdraw at the last moment. The players took part willingly in the festivities that surrounded the event, mingling with guests and celebrities to make them feel welcome. When asked to attend sales conventions in San Diego, Chicago and Miami, there was no hesitation, and six brave, perhaps foolhardy, LPGA star players volunteered to use clubs and balls manufactured by a small Scottish club maker we had signed up for Colgate. Unfortunately, that first step into the golf equipment business was not a wise one!

"With so much talent available to us we put the women golfers in our commercials "plugging" our products, as well as the tournament. Over several years, thirty-five individuals were exposed to the public in this way and that recognition could only enhance the appeal of the player herself, as well as stimulating a desire to watch the event.

"It is true that the raising of the prize money to $110,000 as against the average of $25,000 at that time did not hurt nor did in-store promotions and national television coverage. With the abrupt and never-ending increase in prize money on the men's tour, one is apt to equate contestant's enthusiasm solely to this factor of money to be won. But I believe this is a fallacy. If you don't put on a tournament where the players are the 'stars', not the guests and celebrities, you are on the wrong track. If the players don't look forward to take part in, and to feel part of the event, no amount of money is going to buy their wholehearted support. One can see that the first two "MSFC" events had that support.

"In the first Colgate-Dinah Shore (it was actually titled the Dinah Shore-Colgate) a field of 41 teed-up at Mission Hills on that auspicious Friday, April 14, 1972. 23 players in that field are now active in the MSFC as Founders and Players. Four of that initial group went on to win the Colgate: Mickey Wright in 1973, Jo Ann Prentice in 1974, Sandra Palmer in 1975 and Kathy Whitworth in 1977. Three of these past winners were competing in this year's event, so were Marlene Hagge, Sandra Spuzich and Louise Suggs, celebrating their seventeenth Dinah Shore. JoAnne Carner gave Juli Inkster a run for her money. In 1987, she also finished in second place in the U.S. Women's Open. This goes to show that in this great game of golf there is no time limit as to how long a good player can continue to excel. This longevity is amply demonstrated in the low scores needed to win an event on the men's Senior Tour.

"Marilynn Smith has taken a courageous step in organizing the Founders' Classic. I am sure this is only the forerunner of several tournaments that will begin to feature the 'Senior" women professionals. Sponsors will see that with more and more women taking up golf, and I am not referring just to the college entrant, a viewing public will want to see the star women golfers of yesteryear battling it out and still playing sub-par golf.

"TV coverage will be needed to bring the feats of the Founders and Players into the nation's living rooms, and with four tours to accommodate some ingenuity on the part of the sponsor, golfing authority and TV programmers will be needed. Perhaps not all golf tournaments must be played and televised on Saturdays and Sundays. Viewing of sports is an every day occasion, not just a weekend necessity. Anyway, I will leave that future headache to someone else!

"I wish Marilynn and you other fine golfers who will be teeing-up in October at Prestonwood, good fortune and sincere thanks for the fine memories you have given to me, and others at Colgate when you helped give birth to the Dinah Shore."

Things I Can't Wait to Tell You

In 1958, I was paired with Ben Hogan in the Dallas Civitan Open pro-am. I walked to the first tee with the legend—yes, we played the back tees. I was 29; he was 46. He finished in the Top Ten in 241 of 292 events; I, um, never mind. I didn't know what to expect. There are many myths about Hogan. I can confirm the one about feeling like you were in the presence of royalty when you were with him. It is true. He struck the ball in a way I'd never seen. Or heard. If the course superintendent only mowed a two-foot circle of fairway, he could hit it. We both shot 72. His putting was off that day, but it didn't matter.

I not only got to play golf with Ben Hogan, I got to know Ben Hogan. It was a privilege.

We were in his office one time talking golf and he gave me a tip that has served me well. He said, "If you're not sure whether a shot requires a four-iron or a five-, take the four-iron and choke down." I never forgot it.

•

When I was a kid, Stan Musial was in his prime and I was a big fan. He was my favorite baseball player so you can imagine how excited I was playing alongside Stan, Yogi Berra and Al Lopez, the former manager of the Cleveland Indians and Chicago White Sox, in a pro-am at Sunset Golf Club in Florida. Stan was a southpaw at the plate and on the tee. He hit a few wild shots, let's say they landed in foul territory, but it hardly mattered. It was as close as I'd come to realizing my childhood dream of playing in the majors. Of course, I had to bend Yogi's ear about what a good pitcher I used to be. Imagine a girl bragging about her pitching ability to the guy who caught Don Larsen's perfect World Series game. What was I thinking?

•

Sticking with baseball, I was at the Yankees spring training complex in Florida and met Casey Stengel. I told him I used to be a pretty good pitcher. "You should see my fastball." I said. "I still play catch, my arm's in good shape." He took me up on the offer. I fired a fastball—wearing my baseball glove, high heels and a skirt—for Casey Stengel, the New York Yankees manager. *Really.* I took the ball and looked at the catcher. It was Bill Dickey. I looked a second time to be sure. (Bill caught for the Yankees for 17 years, played in 1,789 games, but never saw a skirt on the mound.) I wound up and fired. Casey, still in uniform, stood behind me, tilted slightly forward in anticipation, his arms folded across his chest— like he expected to discover the Yankees' next 20-game winner. I have a picture to prove it. Unfortunately it was taken before radar guns or I'd tell you more.

•

I met Bobby Thompson, the New York Giants outfielder who hit "the Shot Heard 'Round the World" against the Brooklyn Dodgers to win the 1951 National League playoff series. It was during spring training in St. Petersburg, Florida. We became friends and went on several dates. He was another ballplayer with celebrity status. His fame came from one memorable hit that will be remembered forever.

•

Jack Nicklaus and I played a charity exhibition match in Palm Beach at the Breakers Hotel against Lee Trevino and Shirley Englehorn. He gave me a putting tip that helped us win the match when I rolled in a six-foot birdie putt on the seventeenth hole. I started to play better using Jack's advice and won at Columbus in 1972.

•

Tom Weiskopf was in Columbus in 1972 watching the Pabst Ladies Classic at Riviera Country Club. I can't recall what it was (senior moment) but he gave me a helpful pointer and I gave him credit afterward. He said he was "stunned by the class and abilities of the LPGA gals. These girls can really play, I mean *really*. What gets me, though, is that this lovely woman Marilynn asked me for help. Get this: I watched her play three holes Saturday. She sticks a second shot up two feet to birdie No. 11; she gets a hole-in-one with a perfect three-iron the next shot; then she drives it absolutely dead center about 260 on the next hole. And she wants me to help her!"

I ran into Tom later that day. He shook his head and said, "Now, I've seen it all."

I'm blushing.

My hole-in-one on No. 12 was worth $200. The prize for a hole-in-one on No. 9 was $1,000.

The Pabst Ladies Classic was my last LPGA victory. What a way to go out.

•

In 1973, just before I teed off on the seventh hole at the Colgate Dinah Shore Winners Circle Championship, Roone Arledge, president of ABC-Sports, asked me to do color commentary after I finished my round. He said, "You'll be fine. Men and women are golf experts. Men are commentators at women's tournaments, so why not have a woman do the same at a men's tournament?" I was in the tower at No. 16 with Henry Longhurst, an Englishman. Henry wasn't familiar with many LPGA players. On the other hand, I wasn't familiar with TV. I debuted cold turkey without preparation, without coaching (advantage Longhurst). When Frank Gifford, the lead announcer, asked me to comment on the action at 16 I wasn't sure what to say. The green was clear so I leaned forward to see the tee but my view was blocked. Nobody told me to watch the monitor. Welcome to TV, Marilynn.

I also did color commentary for ABC-TV at the Colonial Men's Invitational in Fort Worth. The broadcasting team had Chris Schenkel and Byron Nelson in the tower at the eighteenth hole; Bill Flemming and I were at No. 16, Dave Marr and Frank Gifford were on the course. This time I was glued to the monitor.

At the 1973 U.S. Open at Oakmont, I was in the tower at No. 16 with Frank Gifford. It was intimidating at first, but Frank let me offer insights and it went smoothly. At least I think it did. After all, that was the Open where Johnny Miller shot 63 in the final round to come from six-shots back and win. My voice may have leaped a few octaves when he made that spectacular run.

A funny incident happened that day. An old friend from Topeka waved to me, made her way past the marshals and climbed up the tower into our booth. She brought our baby pictures with her, taken when we were one-year old toddlers. She handed them to me just as Frank Gifford said, "And, Marilynn, what did you think of that shot?" All I could say was, I'm sorry, Frank, I was looking at baby pictures.

•

In mid-1960, 21,228 golf fans set a McCormick Place attendance record when the PGA Chicago Golf Show featured clinics with Arnold Palmer, Byron Nelson, Dutch Harrison, Mary Mills, Jack Fleck, Johnny Revolta and yours truly. And that was just the first day of a three-day show.

Byron Nelson and I did one of the clinics together. It had to be the largest audience I ever faced.

•

I was fortunate to meet five presidents during my career. I was at Cherry Hills Country Club one day when the President Eisenhower was playing golf. The pro asked if I'd like to meet him. We rode in a golf cart past the security agents. Ike smiled when I introduced myself as Ed Arn's niece. (Ed Arn, the governor of

HAVE CLUBS, WILL TRAVEL

Kansas, made the second nominating speech for General Eisenhower when he ran for president.) That resonated with him and he greeted me with a solid handshake. I noticed his golf ball in the rough under a tree. I wasn't comfortable about suggesting how he should play the shot so I just watched. He hit a low line-drive punch shot that made it to the green. I applauded.

•

The 1960 presidential election took place when I lived in Tequesta, Florida. Ed Ficker, the head pro at Tequesta Country Club knew president-elect John F. Kennedy would be teeing off and invited me to meet him. I went to the first tee and this handsome fellow looked me right in the eye and said, "Hello, nice to meet you." After I wished him well, he teed his ball up and sliced it into the trees on the right.

•

Richard Nixon was vice president the first time I met him. We were at the Plaza Hotel for the Metropolitan Golf Writers dinner. I was the LPGA president at the time and we were together at the head table.

The second time we met was after he became president. I was playing in the Southgate Ladies Open in Prairie Village, Kansas.

209

That same day, I, along with other members of the President's Committee on Physical Fitness, had been invited to be the guest of President Nixon at a dinner in Washington honoring the members of the Olympic team and coaches.

I made it from the course to Washington and back in time for my 12:30 p.m. tee time the next day. I arrived at my hotel about 5:30, jumped into an evening gown and went to the dinner.

I remember being quoted in the paper as saying "I tried to get some rest on the plane trip back, but there were so many interesting people to talk to. I met even more while I waited for my bags at the airport." My gift of gab doesn't have an off switch.

•

Gerald Ford and I were introduced at the Colgate-Dinah Shore Tournament. He loved golf and played as a guest celebrity in many pro-am tournaments. As much as he loved the game, he never mastered it. He was famous for spraying shots everywhere. Bob Hope quipped, "President Ford doesn't know what course he's playing until he sees where his first tee shot lands."

•

I was on the PING staff when George H.W. Bush was inducted into the Texas Golf Hall of Fame. I was at the ceremony and gave him a PING putter.

•

If any co-founder friends are reading this I'd like to quell rumors that I met Washington, Lincoln and Coolidge. Or, that I voted for them.

Somebody, Call 911

Have you ever heard a golfer say, I dodged a bullet out there? It usually means he was down in a match but managed to salvage victory. I, on the other hand, dodged a real a bullet on a golf course during a tournament on a sunny day with birds chirping happily in the trees.

But, first, let me tell you about being robbed four times, once at knifepoint.

I arrived in North Carolina and took a taxi to my hotel. The driver dumped me at the front door and took off. I stood with my suitcase and golf clubs waiting for a bellhop. Suddenly, a man sprinted from the hotel waiving a knife. He grabbed me before I could react, with the blade across my neck and blurted out, "Give me your money." I wasn't about to fumble; I gave him the purse and he fled across a field. A bellhop helped me search for the purse in case he ditched it, but no luck. Once I calmed down I realized I was lucky he didn't slit my throat.

I was robbed twice in Dallas. Both robberies took place while I was teaching. When I got home the front door was open. I was afraid to go in so I called a friend. Several items, mostly jewelry, were missing. I lost a pearl necklace, the one I always wore when I played golf. It was my trademark.

I also lived in Princeton, a Dallas suburb. When I got home from the golf course, both dogs acted disturbed. No wonder, another jewelry thief had robbed me.

Finally, to complete the *Grand Slam of Felonies*, my hotel room was rifled during the Colgate-Dinah Shore Championship. Hotel rooms in Palm Springs were hit two years in a row despite added security precautions. I think the ring of thieves knew we'd be on the golf course from 8:00 a.m. until at least 6:00 p.m. Forty rooms were hit. A newspaper account said I lost 50-60 pieces of jewelry, a tape cassette and a radio from an unlocked suitcase. The police suspected the burglar used a passkey to gain entry.

Back to bullets on the golf course …

It happened at a golf tournament in Florida. I was paired with Australian Margie Masters. We were on No. 14 with out-of-bounds on the left and beyond it, a thick grove of trees. I backed away from a shot because I had second thoughts about my alignment just as a shot rang out. A .45 Magnum bullet zipped past my head—exactly where I had been standing. It penetrated the ground inches from the scorekeeper's foot. We all hit the ground, Margie, our caddies and the scorekeeper. Six or seven shots sprayed out over the golf course.

A priest, Monsignor Kelly, was in the gallery. He came over to find out what happened. I said, "Somebody shot at us." He walked into the trees to investigate, his arms outstretched as if to say, "It's OK, come out and we won't hurt you." No answer. After a long delay and much probing, the tournament director said to resume play. Margie and I were quivering but we managed to finish the round and, somehow, made the cut.

Several months went by. At a tournament in New York, Monsignor Kelly asked if I really wanted to know what happened on the course in Florida. Of course, I did. He invited me to have a drink. I didn't drink but, in retrospect, it would have been a good time to start. His first words were, "Marilynn, you are one lucky girl." There was a sniper hiding in the bushes, deliberately shooting at the golfers. He went after him but the sniper jumped on a motorcycle and got away before the Monsignor could get the license number.

The 21st Century

Things change over the years. Equipment improvements, course conditioning, the extensive tournament training players receive in college, all the golf programs for girls and women—those things didn't exist when I took up the game. Who knew about fitness centers? Clubs weren't built to a tour player's specifications the way they are now. The woman who purchased a set of Spalding Marilynn Smith irons at the May Company was, essentially, getting the same clubs I played with, other than the shaft.

I don't recall anyone hiring a tour caddie in the 1950s and 1960s. Most were local high school kids assigned by the caddie master. They couldn't help with club selection or read greens so they didn't have an impact on our game. In some cases, a caddie may have played the course regularly so his local knowledge could help. For the most part, though, they carried a bag, raked traps and tended pins. If we played a few tournaments in one geographic area we might have the same caddie, but a tour caddie? No, we couldn't afford them. Check that, Alice Bauer Hagge could—she married one, Bob Hagge. But, soon after, the LPGA instituted a rule that family members couldn't caddie. That's not true any more. We did it to avoid criticism lest anybody suggest it afforded the player an unfair advantage.

Skip ahead to the mid-70s in St. Petersburg when a young man named Frank Chilton asked Amy Alcott, a rookie, if he could caddie for her in her third professional tournament. She hired him, won the event, and went on to win Rookie of the Year honors with Frank on the bag—where he remained for a long time. As good a caddie as he was, Frank Chilton never played golf. Not a single hole.

At first, there were just a few women golf commentators. Now, they appear regularly on the course, in the booth and the studio. Judy Rankin, Dottie Pepper, Jane Crafter, Kay Cockerill, Beth Daniel, Donna Caponi, Val Skinner and Mary Bryan, come to mind. Kelly Tilghman is a lead announcer, and is regularly seen in the studio.

We've grown from almost no media coverage to the LPGA signing a 10-year agreement with Golf Channel—when Carolyn Bivens was commissioner in 2010—making it the tour's exclusive cable network. I should also mention that with the influx of Asian players on tour, Carolyn Bivens brought Shirley Chin aboard and the LPGA paid her to help them speak English.

Our players are spotlighted on magazine covers, in print articles, television specials, infomercials, websites, Twitter, Facebook and other social commentary outlets. Think about all the equipment and apparel endorsements, corporate outings, and spokesperson opportunities. Good players these days are mini-conglomerates.

My Favorites

I've been asked many times, "What is your favorite golf course?"

These are the Top Ten courses I've played:

1. Augusta National Golf Club, Augusta, GA

2. Cypress Point Club, Pebble Beach, CA

3. Pebble beach Golf Course, Pebble Beach, CA

4. The Old Course at St. Andrews, Fife, Scotland

5. The Homestead's Cascades Course, Hot Springs, VA

6. The Broadmoor Golf Club, Colorado Springs, CO

7. Pine Valley Golf Club, Pine Valley, NJ

8. St. George's Golf & Country Club, Ontario, Canada

9. Royal Melbourne Golf Club (West), Melbourne, Australian

10. Augusta Country Club, Augusta, GA

World Golf Hall of Fame

The phone call; I couldn't believe it. You never expect it to happen. It was a total surprise. I was so nervous.

I was aware that Renee Powell and Sandra Post who I've known for eons—both are close friends—talked to several people and wrote lots of letters on my behalf.

But you're never prepared—at least I wasn't. My phone rings all the time so I was stunned when it was a conference call from Jack Peter, senior vice president and chief operating officer of the Hall, Eleanor Lanza, director of media relations, and my friend Carol Mann. Jack asked if I was sitting down, and before I could answer he said, "You have been unanimously elected to the World Golf Hall of Fame in the Lifetime Achievement Category."

Then I was told it had to be a secret until the Hall issued a formal announcement, which wouldn't happen for about three weeks. Naturally, I told about 20 people—dialing as fast as I could. One was Kathy Whitworth, who told a few others.

It is the greatest honor I ever received. I hadn't visited the Hall in St. Augustine until I went for my induction ceremony. It was amazing. The lake, the tower, the birds flying around—the whole scene was magic—the sidewalk with the players' names.

Kathy Whitworth was my presenter. I have great respect for her. I've known Kathy since she came on tour. I knew her parents and always made it a point to see them when they followed her on tour.

Inside the Hall is unreal. Exhibits depict the history of so many legends. A man and woman came to my house and picked out memorabilia for my exhibit. Of all things, they took my bible—I thought that was unusual. After my exhibit opened to the public a couple touring the Hall, saw the bible and wrote me a letter. Can you believe it? They thought it was so nice that I am a believer, as they are. They had never seen a bible in such an exhibit. Apparently it is unusual. I was flabbergasted—they are total strangers. I have the letter and hope I'll get to meet them someday.

•

Kathy Whitworth's Presentation Speech

It is my pleasure and privilege to present to you this evening Miss Marilynn Smith for her induction into the World Golf Hall of Fame.

There is no one more deserving of this recognition than Marilynn Smith.

Her contribution to the game as well as being one of the thirteen founders of the LPGA is well documented.

Had it not been for Marilynn and the other twelve founders, the LPGA would not have happened. I think I can speak for all of us who are members of the LPGA when I say thank you for all you've done to give us a chance for a career in golf.

Of the thirteen founders, we are fortunate this evening to have, not only Marilynn, but also three other founders in our audience. Please help me recognize Betty Jameson, Shirley Spork and Louise Suggs. Also, though, not a founder, we have with us Miss Betty Hicks who was there in the beginning and contributed a great deal to the LPGA.

And though Patty Berg is no longer with us, I know she had high regard for Marilynn. In fact, Marilynn was the first recipient of the Patty Berg Distinguished Service Award. And if Patty were here she would definitely be in the front row leading a Standing "O" for Marilynn.

In the beginning of the LPGA things were not easy. The president was the commissioner, and the players had to do all the work. The office and headquarters were in the back of the car. The pressroom was in the parking lot. The locker room was the trunk of the car. Players did the rules, the pairings, set the course, and the

225

treasurer would write the checks on Sunday night. The first check I ever received was $35 and written next to the scoreboard.

But the main responsibility was in the president's hands. She had to negotiate contracts, call sponsors and potential sponsors, make numerous appearances, hold meetings (which at times could be pretty vocal), do most of the public relations ... all the while trying to play tournament golf!

The LPGA was fortunate in the early going to have some great players as our president ... Patty Berg being the first, Babe Zaharias, Louise Suggs and Marilynn Smith.

In visiting with different players who were in that era (including myself), all thought Marilynn did a extraordinary job as president and more than anyone contributed greatly to the success of the tour.

Mickey Wright said she always remembers the hours and hours Marilynn would spend on the phone talking to sponsors, potential sponsors, the press and anyone else she thought might help the Association.

You might say Marilynn always went beyond the call.

In addition to all she was as president, she did manage to win 21 tournaments including two majors. We will never know how many more tournaments she might have won if all her time was devoted to working on her game.

Marilynn turned pro in 1949 and immediately signed a contract with the Spalding Sporting Goods Company, a relationship that would last 27 years. In that span, Marilynn would give literally thousands of clinics, going all over the U.S. and the world. This is when Marilynn began to be considered as the LPGA's Goodwill Ambassador.

In doing these clinics, Marilynn touched a lot of lives, many of them young girls. Two of those young ladies are here this evening: Sandra Post and Renee Powell. They credit Marilynn for their decision to become LPGA players.

Many of us always felt that Marilynn put our best foot forward. She was always a lady, impeccably dressed, wearing a skirt, usually with a sweater, pearl earrings and necklace—always the necklace!!! In your honor, Marilynn, I have mine on tonight!!!

Marilynn always had a smile. No matter how things were going, you could always count on a smile from Marilynn. Some even began to call her "Smiley."

Marilynn Smith

Marilynn was very friendly and always gracious. When I came on tour in 1959, President Marilynn found time to welcome me, and my mother. It meant a lot to me then and still does. She is just great.

1972 turned out to be a very important year. It was the last year Marilynn would win a tournament and the first year for the Colgate Palmolive/Dinah Shore Championship. This started an era that some of us refer to as the Colgate years.

Not only did Colgate sponsor the Dinah Shore, they took the LPGA around the world. We had tournaments in England, Hong Kong, Manila, Singapore, Australia and Kuala Lumpur, just to mention a few. It truly was a wonderful time.

Colgate also asked some of us to do commercials. They asked Marilynn and me to team up for one. I don't know what they said to Marilynn, but they recommended that I keep my day job!!

It was great fun, though, and some of the players were quite good. Laura Baugh appeared in a toothpaste commercial, and it wasn't half bad.

In the 1970s, Marilynn started slowing down her playing career. However, her support and love for the LPGA and women's golf never slowed.

228

She began to turn her energy toward other venues. Just as she helped start the LPGA and the Teaching Division, she started to look for other ways to promote the game.

In 1973, Marilynn did some commentating for the Dinah Shore, the PGA, the U.S. Open and the Colonial.

She organized and conducted 50 Marilynn Smith U.S. and international golf tours, went to Japan for the National Golf Foundation, organized and conducted the first women's senior golf tournament from 1987-1989. I was lucky enough to win the first one and I still wear the beautiful watch given to the winner.

Marilynn is still involved in many charity golf events. From 1994 to 2001, she raised money for the Children's Brain Tumor Foundation. She raised money for the Baylor University golf team from 1994–1999.

She is currently involved with the Marilynn Smith EWGA Classic benefiting the Marilynn Smith Scholarship and LPGA Girl's Golf.

As you can see, Marilynn is tireless in promoting the game. She is the Energizer Bunny.

A quote from Mark Johnson of the Dallas Morning News: *"Though she made some money and won some trophies, what she gave us is more important than what she took."*

In 1999, Frank Luksa of the Dallas Morning News wrote, *"The LPGA should reach into its history, find its pioneers and pay tribute to them while they're still here and bask in the applause.*

And so, with your applause tonight, please welcome Miss Marilynn Smith to the World Golf Hall of Fame.

Karsten and the Solheim Cup

I was associated with PING (Karsten Manufacturing Company) for eighteen years and proudly promoted their products. In fact, I was the first lady pro to use a PING putter.

I met Karsten Solheim when he was designing the first PING putter—in his garage. What an innovator, there were tools everywhere. He handed me a putter and said, "What do you think?" At first glimpse you would have thought he was playing a trick. I said, "It's different." My voice may have trembled—it *sure* was different.

He explained the laws of physics and mechanics—how and why he made the radical design. It was a total departure from putters I'd seen or used. It was heel-toe weighted. And offset. Then there was the color, I'm not sure if it was brass or bronze. I later found out it was brass, but he changed it to some sort of bronze. The putter had so many new features. How about the "PING" it made when it struck the ball? The name, alone, was genius.

Karsten gave me a putter and it helped me. Before that, I putted with a Bullseye for years, but I was never a particularly good putter. Short putts gave me fits. From six-feet in I battled a tendency to aim left and had trouble finding a putter I could aim properly. I was the first woman to try putting left-hand low like Johnny Pott. I played with him in the Haig & Haig Mixed Foursome Championship and he was deadly. I won the $10,000 St. Petersburg Florida Open putting left hand low. But people said, "Gosh, you look funny!" and I didn't want to look funny so I went back to my old putting style.

After PING Eye2 irons revolutionized the equipment market, Karsten enjoyed celebrity but was low-key about it. He'd stand under a shade tree at major tournaments—his little white beard gave him away—and draw examples with a pencil on a small pad as he explained his club's characteristics for anybody who cared to learn.

He was both innovator and maverick. Players who used PING clubs were paid after the season based on their performance. Unlike other manufacturers who signed players and paid them up front, he felt that PING players should *want* to use PING equipment.

I've known the Solheim family for years. They are reputable; have done an enormous amount for the game; and have been generous LPGA supporters. The Solheim Cup sits at the peak of their mountain.

In 1990, when Karsten's family and company agreed to sponsor the Solheim Cup they, along with the LPGA and the Women Professional Golfers' European Tour had a common desire to showcase women's golf, globally. Karsten and Louise Solheim insisted that PING would be a background player. As Louise put it, "The formidable abilities of these talented lady professional golfers and the countries they represented would take center stage. The fact that PING was there to showcase the event was to be minimized. We would feature great golf amid patriotic pomp and circumstance."

They, admittedly, had no idea what the event would mean to women's golf. The format mirrors the Ryder Cup, but the Ryder Cup took a half-century to gain traction. Well, it didn't take the ladies long. From day one, players on both sides focused on qualifying for the team. They watch their point standings every week. The ultimate goal is to represent their country on a worldwide stage.

The Europeans quickly matched the favored Americans and the Solheim Cup blossomed into a competitive series. Karsten knew it was important for the world to watch so he made sure the matches are properly televised.

I found out, first hand, what the tournament's energy level is like. In 2007, Louise Suggs and I raised the American flag at the opening ceremony at Halmstad Golf Club in Halmstad, Sweden.

Karsten was born in Norway so playing the matches in a Scandinavian country was very special to the family.

The gallery's spirit is comparable to the energy at a Super Bowl: patriotic chants, flag-waving, team apparel worn by thousands of spectators, at a *golf tournament*. It takes laryngitis and fatigue to quiet things down at day's end.

Betsy King captained the United States team, Helen Alfredsson, the European team. The United States retained the cup, defeating Europe 16–12. Many were startled when the final day singles matches turned into a United States rout. The U.S. won the singles 8-1/2 to 3-1/2. The Brits called it a dust-up.

The Solheim Cup matches have matured; the chemistry is there. It's a runaway best seller and all of golf is better for it.

The RR Donnelley Founders Cup

The 2011 inaugural RR Donnelley Founders Cup was played at Wildfire Golf Club in Phoenix as a tribute to the 13 LPGA co-founders.

RR Donnelley has been generous in supporting the LPGA. The best women golf professionals in the world participate which lends credibility to the event's importance. The tournament is steeped in history. Three living founders still attend to support today's players and act as ambassadors for the organization.

The inaugural format was distinctive in that the winners received no cash prize money. The players agreed to donate the entire $1 million purse to charity, a first in LPGA history—possibly in golf history. Half was donated to general charities, the other half to charities chosen by the top-10 finishers. In 2012, a regular cash purse was paid the winners. Karrie Webb won the inaugural event in 2011; Yani Tseng won in 2012.

We sit behind the eighteenth green each day and the players end their round by stopping by to shake hands and say thank you for giving them the opportunity to play professional golf. I feel uplifted and humble. I marvel at the LPGA's success and I'm extremely proud that we fought to pave the way for women's golf. We didn't give up when times were tough.

I can't say enough about my admiration for Chief Executive Officer Tom Quinlan of RR Donnelley & Sons Company. He and his company play such a vital role. You may be curious (I certainly was) about the way a great corporate relationship comes about. He graciously explained it this way:

"My chance encounter in 2009 with interim commissioner Marty Evans at a business conference led to our partnership and RR Donnelley's designation as the "Official Print Provider of the LPGA". However, a great pro-am experience between John Paloian, our chief operating officer, and other senior managers with Wendy Ward really cemented the relationship and led us to consider a larger commitment.

"The LPGA and its new Commissioner, Mike Whan, proposed a handful of title sponsorship opportunities but the one that resonated most with us was the Founders Cup. A new tournament that would pay fitting tribute to the 13 pioneering women who founded the LPGA and where players would uniquely donate the entire event purse to charities of their choice with a major commitment to the LPGA-USGA Girls Golf program.

"The inaugural RR Donnelley Founders Cup in 2011 exceeded our company's and our customers' expectations. We were honored to meet and spend a week getting to know three of the living Founders, including "Miss Personality" Marilynn Smith. The people of Phoenix and worldwide television viewers were treated to an exciting tournament and a deserving first champion in Karrie Webb.

"RR Donnelley rewarded the year-one selflessness of the LPGA players by agreeing to a full purse for the 2012 event while continuing the major donation to the LPGA-USGA Girls Golf program and launching the season-long RR Donnelley "Scoring for Schools" effort. The #1 player in the world, Yani Tseng, bested a stellar field in 2012 and feedback from the media and participating customers could not be more positive.

"RR Donnelley is proud to continue honoring the past, showcasing the present and providing for the future of women's golf."

The LGPA Foundation's Marilynn Smith Scholarship

In 2004, I moved to Phoenix. I always wanted to live in the west where the lifestyle is fabulous. Due to an injury from skiing and knees that have been overworked, I can no longer play golf. I had to swap my golf club for a cane. But I'm still involved in my local golf community, occasionally giving golf instruction, speaking at events and working zealously to raise money for the Marilynn Smith Scholarship Fund.

Drawing on my experience at the University of Kansas in 1948 when there was no formal program for female golfers, I established a scholarship fund to assist young women golfers with the help of Dr. Betsy Clark and Sherry Greene at LPGA headquarters.

Scholarships are granted annually through the LPGA Foundation and the Marilynn Smith Scholarship Fund. The objective is to provide assistance to female high school seniors who have played golf in high school or in their community and are planning to play golf at an accredited college or university in the United States.

The Marilynn Smith LPGA Charity Golf Classic is held in the fall each year at Pebblecreek Golf Course in Goodyear, Arizona (a

Phoenix suburb). We play a pro-am scramble so the amateurs get to hit the same shots as their professional playing partners.

The tournament committee works tirelessly, year-round planning the event, soliciting sponsors and silent auction donations and selling raffle tickets. Last year, thirty-one LPGA tour players and teaching professionals were paired with men and women amateurs.

 I'd like to share a story about Vivian Bucknam, a nurse who lived in an apartment in New York City. She was a social golfer who loved the LPGA. Sandra Post and I were her favorite touring pros and she always made it a point to be in the gallery when we played in New England. I noticed her now and then, her face seemed familiar, but I didn't know her name or anything about her. She hadn't said hello, or attempted to make eye contact. Well, one time I was in a hotel restaurant eating breakfast and she was nearby at another table. God must have said, "Look who's here, go say hello." I introduced myself and we had a delightful conversation that ultimately led to a lifelong friendship.

Vivian even went to New Zealand and the Dominican Republic on golf tours I led—the ones Dick Bigelow and I set up. Not long ago, Vivian passed away at age 92. In her will she bequeathed $200,000 to the Marilynn Smith Scholarship Fund. The gift was unexpected. Her donation helped us give $10,000 scholarships to ten young women golfers who needed tuition assistance.

You never know when something like that will happen. I tell donors their contribution may benefit another Babe, Nancy, or Annika—a budding talent who can't afford college. How great would it be to track her college career and some day see her name atop the leader board at a tour event? It's something to think about because, you never know.

The Rewards of a Scholarship

Georgi Salant, a Marilynn Smith scholarship winner in 2010, wrote to me recently. Letters like this make it all worthwhile.

Dear Marilynn,

 I thought you might like an update about my golf and school this past year. I just finished my second year at Williams College and it was another amazing year. I finally declared my major in chemistry but also found myself taking some great classes like Roman archaeology and astronomy.

The tight-knit community at Williams makes me want to always be there and this summer I am excited to be doing chemistry research.

In terms of golf, I am happy to say that the Williams women's golf team had a great year. We were undefeated in the fall season, winning all five tournaments and we placed in the top three in each of our spring tournaments, finishing with a win in the last tournament. The biggest highlight of the year was our fifth place finish at the NCAA tournament—our best finish, ever. It is great to be making an impact on my team and to be playing the game I love.

I want to thank you so much for your scholarship as it has helped me further my education. I really appreciate your friendship so much and hope everything is well.

Warmly,
Georgi

Lindsay Schneider played collegiate golf at the University of North Dakota from 1999–2003. She graduated with am Accounting degree and passed the CPA exam. She is married and has two children.

Dear Marilynn,

I was honored to be the first Marilynn Smith Scholarship recipient. It allowed me to pursue my passion for golf at college while focusing on my academic studies. You are a role model to so many women golfers. I was fortunate to meet you in Texas during the NCAA Division II National Tournament and staying in touch through the years has made me realize that the scholarship was more than a down payment for college. It was about a lifelong relationship with someone who has done and continues to do so much for women's golf. You are genuinely passionate about the game and those you surround yourself with.

Lindsay Schneider

Tips, Advice, Remedies, Fixes and Counseling

The least I can do is leave you with a few golf tips. No, you don't have to find a persimmon driver. My friends and I can help your game no matter what kind of clubs you play.

I called on a wide range of pros and instructors—folks who have different ways of expressing themselves—because it's not necessarily *what* instructors say, as much as *how* they say it. I've also included tips that have been in my files for many years—because they helped me. Hopefully, they will help you, too.

OK, here we go. Clear the furniture out of the way; watch out for light fixtures and floral arrangements on your backswing.

•

Here's a tip I learned years ago from Joe Norwood, the legendary teaching pro at the Los Angeles Country Club. It produces a low chip-and-run shot with plenty of over spin that's accurate and easy to control:

The key is in your grip. Take a strong, three-knuckle grip with your left hand (you want to be able to see the first three knuckles) and weaken your right hand grip by rotating your hand counterclockwise on the club. Be sure the "V" of your right hand points to the left of your chin—you should see creases at the base (back side) of your right wrist.

That's it! This slight adjustment locks your wrists so you can't flip them through impact. Just be sure to set up with the ball back in your stance and your weight on your left leg.

Try this drill to help you get the right feel: Swing a club with just your right arm, keeping a constant gap between the butt end of the shaft and your right forearm. Practice and you'll eliminate chops, tops and chili-dips from your chipping repertoire.

•

Arnold Palmer was delighted to pass on a bit of assistance:

"The swing is the easiest part of golf. Rule No. 1 regarding the swing is to take the club back smoothly, and without breaking your wrists. Do this for the first 12 inches the clubhead moves and you've got the swing practically licked.

"Starting the club this way gets your entire body into the act. You have to use your leg muscles, your torso muscles, and your shoulders. Your body gets started on a nice, easy, well-coordinated pattern of motion from feet to shoulders."

•

Shirley Spork, LPGA Master Pro—one of the best teachers anywhere, and my dear friend—offers advice on how to practice:

"Tips for straighter, more consistent golf shots.

"CENTER your attention to the ball. Turn your body away from the ball and turn your body back past the ball position.

"SWING freely allowing a complete flow of body energy with weight transfer—from right foot to left foot

"HOLD the finish position until the ball lands near its target.

"The key words to review before each practice shot with a full swing are: Center, Swing, Hold."

•

Former LPGA player, Barbara Romack, stresses rhythm on short shots:

"This is important: Keep both hands working together—at the same speed—as the club goes through the ball. Whether you contact the ball with the back of your left hand or the palm of the right hand is personal preference. Either is correct as long as it is comfortable.

"Short shots are flubbed when the left hand stops abruptly before the clubhead meets the ball.

"Practice. Get the feeling that both hands work in unison, rhythmically, as you swing your wedge through the grass and sand."

•

Sharon Miller played the LPGA tour for 15 years. She is the national head teaching golf professional for the Bird Golf Academy. Sharon discusses perfect posture. Many amateurs lack correct posture at address because they don't understand it. They tend to hunch over:

"Assuming correct posture at address, then maintaining it throughout the swing helps you build a 'coil' of power; helps you stay level; lets you deliver a powerful, balanced swing.

"Step up to the ball and stand straight. Now, *flex* your body *forward from the hip joints.*

"Your spine will be on a much straighter angle than if you bend from the waist. THERE IS A DIFFERENCE. Your hips will be back behind you. Your butt will stick out (watch the touring pros on TV and you'll see it, repeatedly).

"Flex your knees so the spine keeps the same straight angle. Your weight will be over your arches, not your toes.

"Stay level when you swing.

"Drill: Hold a club against your spine—one end on your tailbone, the other on your upper back. If it touches all the way, your spine is straight."

•

Patty Berg taught clinics for decades, always stressing three things:

"CONFIDENCE. One of the most important things to have going for us is confidence. We must learn to be confident when we step up to the ball, fully believing the shot we are about to hit will come off. If we are confident, it WILL come off.

"CONCENTRATION. We have to concentrate when we play golf. Do you ever wonder why things go along so well and then, suddenly, everything goes wrong? You've lost concentration. When the mind gets tired or strays, we lose concentration.

"PATIENCE. The third vital emotion is patience. We must have the will and ability to wait, to endure without complaint. Have the patience to be steady and persevering. Know that everything is going to work just fine."

•

Sandra Spuzich played the LPGA tour for three decades. Her first victory was the 1966 U.S. Open. Here is her "heads up" tip:

"'Keep your head down' is a familiar golf phrase. This is a better idea: Keep your eye on the ball with your chin up. Your shoulders will turn more freely. (Try turning your shoulders with your chin on your chest. Then, lift your chin and try it again.)

"If you keep your head down and your swing is restricted, it often results in topped shots. You 'come up' on the shot because there is less room to swing.

"Next time you practice or play, keep this phrase in mind: "Chin up.'"

•

Former LPGA player Jo Ann Prentice lives in Tucson, AZ where she is co-owner of Golf Stop, a high-tech club fitting and club making company. She wants to help improve your putting:

"Many people think the left hand is dominant in putting. I believe the right hand should supply feel for distance as well as controlling the stroke.

"Take the putter back, low to the ground with the right hand, and push it through with the right hand. You will have a better chance of making the ball roll.

"When you make the ball roll, with a good feel for distance, there are three ways it can go in the hole: over the front lip, or from either side. A firmly hit ball can only go in one way—dead center."

•

Deb Vangellow, an LPGA Master Professional, teaches in Sugar Land TX. She is national vice president of the LPGA Teaching & Club Professionals, and a long-time lead instructor in the LPGA National Education Program. Some golfers lift their left heel on the backswing, others don't. Deb is a "left heel specialist" (just kidding) who explains the effect of lifting your left heel:

"Lifting your heel' on the backswing is okay. If the left heel detaches near the top of the backswing, it results from your upper body coiling. The coil pulls the hip upward and causes an upward pull on the lower left leg and foot.

251

"Detaching and replanting your left heel promotes good movement sequence, and good footwork—the benchmark of champions in all sports. We feel much of our rhythm through our feet. Most golfers make a better energy transfer, as well."

•

Bettye Mims Danoff, rest her soul, was an LPGA co-founder. I used to hit the ball a long way, partially because I used Bettye's strength tip:

"This tip helped me add distance and accuracy. It prevented my hands from opening at the top of my backswing. If the hands open, the tendency is to throw, or cast the club from the top.

"When you take your grip, you should feel the fatty part of the inside of the right thumb press on the left thumb. Be sure you have the same feeling at the top of your backswing—before you start down.

"Keep this in mind, it may give you a little pause a the top which is important. It prevents rushing, before the backswing is completed.

"Women need strong hands. You can build hand strength by squeezing a rubber ball. You can also wet a large hand towel and wring it out, repeatedly. Do that many times, each day. It may make a difference."

•

Nan Ryan is a top teacher. She is the founder and executive director of Pepsi Little People's Golf Championships, the third largest junior golf tournament in the world. Nan wants to help improve your sand play:

"When your ball is in a bunker, you want to be confident that you can: A) Get out; B) Get on the green; C) Get close to the hole.

"Sometimes, the best shot is not toward the hole (example: if the ball is under the lip of the bunker).

"Use a sand wedge for most bunker shots, especially in soft sand. Use a pitching wedge or lofted club if the sand is wet and coarse, or if you have a buried lie.

"Use your normal grip, but place your hands slightly lower on the grip than with regular shots.

"Open your stance and dig your toes into the sand. Position the ball off the heel of your forward foot. The clubface should be slightly open, EXCEPT if the ball is buried. If it's buried, change to a lower lofted club and close the face.

"Swing the club back along your shoulder line, cocking the wrists quickly. Be careful; make sure the club doesn't touch the sand before or during the backswing.

"For longer explosion shots, play the ball back of center, take less sand, and change to a pitching wedge or eight-iron. FINISH THE SWING. Make sure the club keeps moving—accelerating—through the ball with a full finish.

Exception: if you have a buried lie and are using a lower lofted club with a closed face, it's hard to make a full finish. Try for as much as you can. The ball will come out low and rolling."

•

This is an interesting tip from Gerda Boykin, Germany's first woman professional golfer. She played a limited LPGA schedule in the 1960s. I bet this tip helps you:

"Suppose you have a problem missing greens from 100 yards in. Instead of hitting a full short iron, take one club MORE, grip down and make a three-quarter swing. You will be amazed how much straighter the ball flies.

"Remember: One club more, grip down, shorter swing. Less chance for error, more accuracy."

•

More good advice, this time from Jerilyn Britz who played the LPGA tour for 26 years. You have probably seen tour players muscle the ball out of deep rough. Jerilyn talks about deep grass around the greens. Her technique may fool you, but it works:

"When the ball is 'buried' in deep grass around the green, or in the deep rough within a pitching wedge or sand wedge distance from the green, take a very firm grip on the club, and swing in SUPER SLOW motion throughout the stroke—from start to finish.

"Keep your wrists firm through impact—you don't want any 'hitting' action. The ball will come out high and soft."

Surprised?

•

Helen Dettweiler, a co-founder of the LPGA, played the tour in the 1950s and 1960s, then became a teaching pro. Her advice has as much merit today as it did back then:

"Your hands are the only part of your body that touches the club. If you use them correctly, you're on the way to a good swing.

"Grip the club firmly, but relax your body and muscles. Don't take a death grip, it may feel strong, but will actually cause loss of clubhead speed.

"Allow your left wrist to turn (not roll) along an inside path on your backswing. Be sure your left hand is in control at the top of your backswing.

"Try to envision the start of your downswing following the path of your backswing.

"Don't try to hit *at* the ball. Allow the ball to be struck as part of your arc. The resultant swing will be more fluid—not jerky or forced."

•

Betty Hicks played the LPGA tour in the 1950s and later became a golf coach and teacher. She offered advice about club selection:

"High-handicap players are often confused about club selection for approach shots. I'd like to emphasize a simple solution.

"If you have more distance between the ball and the edge of the green than between the edge of the green and the cup, select a lofted club. A pitching wedge is preferred. Lacking a pitching wedge, use a nine-iron.

"If there is less distance between the ball and the edge of the green than between the edge of the green and the hole, select a club with less loft. A seven-iron or six-iron are the best choices for this chip shot.

"More distance to the green, more loft. Less distance, less loft."

•

Linda Volstedt, the former Arizona State University golf coach captured six NCAA titles during her 19 seasons at ASU. She is also a LPGA T&CP Class A Life member.

Add to all that, the ASU women's golf team traditionally ranks among the best in both academics and athletics. Linda's colleagues have bestowed numerous honors on her. Linda wants to pass on some of her favorite expressions; she calls them "Coach V's Thoughts":

"There are no mistakes, only learning experiences. What did you learn today, what can you do better tomorrow?

"Ask for what you want, not what you don't want.

"If you look for what's wrong, you will find it. If you look for what's right, you will find it, also.

"Only discuss or think about your good shots. The others are simply learning experiences.

"PATIENCE increases the odds of something good happening. BELIEVE that things will eventually go your way.

"LUCK is the favor of those who are prepared."

•

Three time U.S. Women's Open champion, Susie Maxwell Berning, is an excellent teacher. Get your putter. Find a place in your carpet that doesn't have a severe break and follow Susie's advice:

"The most important fundamental of putting is keeping the blade square. Set up over the ball and create an imaginary line that runs from the hole back to and through the ball. The objective is to take the putter back on the line, and stroke it through the line to the target with the blade absolutely square to the line at all times.

"Start the stroke by pushing the putter back with the left hand; keep the left wrist firm. The blade should go back low to the ground. This results in a solid hit and rolls the ball better. Do not start the putter back with the right hand—it will lead to a jerky stroke and the right hand will roll over the left (pronate) and break down your firm left wrist.

"Returning to the ball, hit the putt with your right hand and guide with the left along the target line. Your right hand hits against a firm left wrist, with the arms moving through toward the hole.

"The best way to be consistent and accurate is to have a smooth stroke by taking the putter back slowly, then swinging and accelerating through the ball."

•

Former LPGA Championship winner, Shirley Englehorn, won the Teacher of the Year award from the LPGA's Teaching and Club Professional Division. She also won the Ben Hogan Award for her comeback to golf after severe injury. If you tend to be mechanical, Shirley is here to help:

"Golfers tend to be too mechanical. Golf books, videos, articles and televised instruction let you see and learn how to hit shots. But few actually experience the feel of a solidly hit shot, one that comes squarely off the clubface.

"If you learn to hit the ball solidly, length and accuracy will lower your scores. I want to help you visualize and create solid shots.

"Take a five-iron, for example. Practice with it until you are able to make solid contact. Hit high shots and low shots with the same club. Imagine an obstacle, a tree, between you and the target. To go over the tree, position the ball forward in your stance. It will give it a higher trajectory and less roll when it lands. To hit it under the tree, place the ball back in your stance. It gives the ball a lower trajectory and more roll when it lands.

"This learning method allows you to use your imagination so you can create the best shot for a given situation."

•

Linda Craft of the Craft-Zavichias Golf School helped her students relieve tension:

"Take it nice and easy, please, as you set up to the golf ball. You will benefit by remaining tension free. Address the ball with a light grip and soft arms.

"A golf club weighs less than a glass of water. Why grip it tightly? There is no need to have a rigid left arm, either.

"Instead, set up with soft arms, forming a "Y" from your shoulders to the club. The light grip and soft arms allow you to easily hinge your hands on the backswing creating a power source for clubhead speed through the impact."

•

Former LPGA touring pro and major championship winner, Joyce Ziske-Malison, offers alignment advice:

"Alignment is critical if you want to hit a perfect shot. Many golfers aim to the right of their target without realizing it.

"The best way to properly align yourself is to approach from behind the ball, then square the clubface to the target. Finally, take your stance. Don't take your stance first. Don't use your shoulders for alignment.

"You can check your alignment by putting a club on the ground across your toes. Then, step back and see where the club points. It should be the same distance between the ball and your toes, left of the target.

"Practice alignment. Straighter shots will make you a happy golfer."

•

Barbra Crawford-O'Brien is an LPGA Master Professional, and a proponent of visualizing your shots:

"When you stand behind the ball, preparing to align a shot, visualize the shot you want to create so your sub-conscious knows what to do.

"See the ball travel the way you want it to fly—high or low; shaped to the left or right; straight at the target.

"Keep that picture in mind at address and swing to the target."

Career Highlights

1958-1960 – President of the LPGA

1959 – Founded the LPGA Teaching Division, known as the LPGA T&CP with Shirley Spork, Betty Hicks and Barbara Rotvig.

21 LPGA tournament victories, including two majors: Titleholders Championship (1963 and 1964).

1973 – First female television commentator at a men's golf tournament (1973 U.S. Open and The Colonial).

1979 – First recipient of Patty Berg Award for distinguished service to women's golf.

1983 – Golf Digest LPGA Founders Cup for charitable service off the course.

1987 – Vince Lombardi "Distinguished Champions Award."

1987-1989 – Organized the Marilynn Smith Founders' Classic, the first senior women's professional golf tournament held in Dallas, Texas.

66 - Lowest career round shot at the 1964 Titleholders

Five career holes-in-one.

Conducted more than 4,000 golf clinics and seminars for over 250,000 people

Competed in more than 500 tournaments.

1991 – Inducted into the Kansas Golf Hall of Fame.

1994 – Inducted into the Texas Golf Hall of Fame.

1999 – Inducted into the Kansas University Sports Hall of Fame.

2000 – Inducted into the Kansas Sports Hall of Fame.

2000 - One of the six inaugural inductees into the LPGA Teaching and Club Professional (T&CP) Hall of Fame.

2002 – Mercedes-Benz Legends of Women's Golf Award.

2005 – Inducted into the Wichita Sports Hall of Fame and Wichita East High School Sports Hall of Fame.

2006 – Recipient of the Pinnacle Award.

2006 – World Golf Hall of Fame – Lifetime Achievement Category.

2007 – Recipient of the Linda Vollstedt Award.

Marilynn Smith Career Victories

(Date, Tournament, Location, Winning share, Winning score)

July, 1954 Fort Wayne Open, Orchard Ridge CC, Fort Wayne, Indiana, $700; (216)

August, 1955 Heart of America Open, Oakwood CC, Kansas City, Missouri, $900; (220)

September, 1955 Mile High Open, Lakewood CC, Denver, Colorado, $900; (221)

July, 1957 Hot Springs 4-Ball, With Fay Crocker, Hot Springs Shrine Club, Hot Springs, Virginia, $1,500; (281) ** (Unofficial event)

March 2, 1958 Jacksonville Open, Hyde Park Golf Club, Jacksonville, Florida $875; (299)

September, 1959 Memphis Open, Ridgeway CC, Memphis, Tennessee, $1,250; (295)

January, 1962 Naples Pro-Am with Mickey Wright, Naples Golf and Beach Club, Naples, Florida, $612; (143) ** (Unofficial event)

April, 1962 Sunshine Open, Miami Springs, Fla., $1,200; (214)

August, 1962 Waterloo Open, Sunnyside CC, Waterloo, Iowa, $1,200; (279)

April, 1963 Titleholders Championship, Augusta CC, Augusta, Georgia, $1,235; (292)

May, 1963 Peach Blossom Open, Spartanburg CC, Spartanburg, South Carolina, $1,200; (216)

September, 1963 Eugene Ladies' Open, Eugene CC, Eugene, Oregon, $1,350; (295)

November, 1963 Cavern City Open, Riverside CC, Carlsbad, New Mexico, $1,200; (212)

April, 1964 Titleholders Championship, Augusta CC, Augusta, Georgia, $1,300; (289)

August, 1964 Albuquerque Pro-Am, Paradise Hills CC, Albuquerque, New Mexico, $1,350; (216)

April, 1965 Peach Blossom Open, Spartanburg CC, Spartanburg, South Carolina, $1,275; (213)

March, 1966 St. Petersburg Women's Open, Sunset G&CC, St. Petersburg, Florida, $1,650; (285)

March, 1966 Louise Suggs Delray Beach Invitational, Delray Beach CC, Delray Beach, Florida, $1,275; **(211)**

March, 1967 St. Petersburg Orange Classic, Sunset GC, St. Petersburg, Florida, $1,875; **(283)**

May, 1967 Babe Zaharias Open, Bayou Din GC, Beaumont, Texas, $1,500; **(210)**

April, 1968 O'Sullivan Open, Winchester GC, Winchester, Virginia, $1,875; **(216)**

October, 1970 Women's Golf Charities Open, Inwood Forest CC, Houston, Texas, $2,625; **(214)**

August, 1972 Pabst Ladies Classic, Riviera CC, Columbus, Ohio, $4,500; **(210)**

Amateur Victories

1946, 1947 and 1948 Kansas Women's Amateur (1946 at age 17)

1949 Women's National Intercollegiate Golf Tournament

LPGA Annual Money Leaders

1950 – Babe Zaharias $ 14,800

1951 – Babe Zaharias   15,087

1952 – Betsy Rawls   14,505

1953 – Louise Suggs   19,816

1954 – Patty Berg   16,011

1955 – Patty Berg   16,492

1956 – Marlene Hagge   20,235

1957 – Patty Berg   16,272

1958 – Beverly Hanson   12,639

1959 – Betsy Rawls   26,774

1960 – Louise Suggs   16,892

1961 – Mickey Wright   22,236

1962 – Mickey Wright   21,641

1963 – Mickey Wright   31,269

1964 – Mickey Wright   29,800

1965 – Kathy Whitworth   28,658

1966 – Kathy Whitworth   33,517

1967 – Kathy Whitworth   32,937

1968 – Kathy Whitworth   48,379

1969 – Carol Mann   49,152

1970 – Kathy Whitworth   30,235

1971 – Kathy Whitworth   41,181

1972 – Kathy Whitworth   65,063

1973 – Kathy Whitworth   82,864

1974 – JoAnne Carner   87,094

1975 – Sandra Palmer   76,374

1976 – Judy Rankin   150,734

1977 – Judy Rankin   122,890

1978 – Nancy Lopez   189,814

1979 – Nancy Lopez   197,489

•

2011 – Yani Tseng $2,921,713